Su...
F. ...   ...ly.

Td. Ox. 772624

Basic Concepts in
Micro Economics

BASIC CONCEPTS IN MICRO-ECONOMICS

Neil Fuller

B.Sc., M.Sc., M.Inst. P.S.

Checkmate/Arnold

© Checkmate Publications 1984/1985

First published in Great Britain 1984 by
Checkmate Publications,
4 Ainsdale Close, Bromborough, Wirral L63 0EU.

Reprinted with revisions 1985

Edward Arnold (Publishers) Ltd.,
41 Bedford Square, London WC1B 3DQ

Edward Arnold (Australia) Pty Ltd.,
80 Waverley Road, Caulfield East,
Victoria 3145, Australia

Edward Arnold, 3 East Read Street,
Baltimore, Maryland 21202, USA.

All rights reserved. No part of this publication
may be reproduced or transmitted in any form
or by any means, without the written
permission of the Publisher.

ISBN 0 946973 31 8

Text set in 10/12pt Times by Birkenhead Press Ltd. and
Merseyside Graphics Ltd.

Printed and bound by Richard Clay (The Chaucer Press),
Bungay, Suffolk

INTRODUCTION

This book is intended to assist students in the early stages of an economics course to understand some of the basic concepts involved in the subject, although it may also prove useful as a revision aid. Experience has shown that students frequently have difficulty at the outset where the issues are clouded by an excess of data and empirical results, although this is essential at a later stage. The objective here is therefore to produce a concise text which explains in simple terms the concepts involved. Having understood these concepts they should utilise other texts which take a more empirical approach, or the text could be supplemented with information provided by the teacher/lecturer during class exercises and data response work. The book covers the requirements in Micro Economics for an A level course, but will also be useful to students studying for the foundation stages of professional examinations, first year degree courses, and graduate conversion courses.

Neil Fuller

CARTOONS BY GRAHAM DAVIES

CONTENTS

Chapter 1
BASIC CONCEPTS

1.   Economics is the study of how man can provide for his material well-being. As such it analyses the ways in which man can apply his skills, efforts and knowledge to the available natural resources in order to produce those goods and services which will satisfy his wants.

2.   Economics is a Social Science. Social because it studies man and society, although unlike other social sciences it studies only one aspect of man's behaviour; and Science because of the method of study. Economics attempts wherever possible to adopt a scientific approach. Therefore it attempts to use only positive statements which are those which can be verified by appeal to the facts, rather than normative statements, which are frequently matters of opinion, or **VALUE JUDGEMENTS,** about which we may all hold different, but equally valid, opinions. Value judgements are more a matter for policy makers to decide in line with their perception of society's preferences, whilst economists are more concerned with finding the most efficient, or lowest cost, method of achieving a given objective. It cannot be ignored however that inevitably economic decisions will be influenced indirectly by social and political considerations.

Unlike other scientists, however, the economist cannot experiment as it is not possible to have a control experiment. In order to compensate for the lack of control over other variables economists frequently include the expression Ceterus Paribus (Cet. Par.), meaning "other things being equal", when they make a statement, which means that they believe the statement to be true provided other factors remain unchanged.

3.   As resources are always limited in supply and man's wants appear to be insatiable then he always requires more goods than are available. As resources are limited and wants are insatiable man is continually forced to make **CHOICES.** It is the making of these choices which is central to the study of economics. Every time we make a decision to produce something we choose to forego the alternative which we could have produced, the cost of this foregone alternative is known as the **OPPORTUNITY COST.** Opportunity

cost also applies every time we make a decision to buy something as consumers, and every time we make a collective decision as a nation; for example if we produce Concorde those resources will not be available to build roads or hospitals.

4. **SCARCITY** therefore forces us to make **CHOICES,** and as we make choices we are forced to **SACRIFICE** other things, in other words we are forced to **ECONOMISE.** Normally however the choice is not between one good or another, but how many more of one good should we have and how much less of another. Scarcity and choice are therefore central to the study of economics. Those goods which are produced from our scarce resources are referred to as **ECONOMIC GOODS,** and as they are scarce they have a **PRICE**; the price being relative to their scarcity. Goods or resources which are not scarce but are available in unlimited quantities do not have a price, e.g. air; there is no need therefore to economise with them, and so they do not enter the study of economics.

5. Wants can be satisfied by the production of either tangible goods or the enjoyment of services. In the study of economics anything which satisfies a want is said to have **UTILITY.** Different goods however produce different amounts of utility, or the same good can produce different amounts of utility in different places or at different times, for example water has a different utility in a dry country than in Britain.

6. As goods are produced they are then consumed and the act of consumption provides the required utility, but in so doing creates a new want. There is therefore an endless round of production, consumption, and the creation of new wants leading to new production. The rate at which goods are consumed however differs.

6.1 **CONSUMER GOODS** are consumed over a relatively short time period and we receive utility direct from their use, for example shoes. 'Single-use' consumer goods are consumed immediately, for example an ice-cream.

6.2 **CONSUMER DURABLES** yield utility over a longer time period, for example a refrigerator or washing machine. The utility received is not from the good itself but from the stream of services it yields over its lifetime.

6.3 **PRODUCER GOODS** or **CAPITAL GOODS** do not directly satisfy wants, but do so indirectly. They are the plant and machinery acquired by firms for the purpose of producing other goods which may produce utility. As such they constitute the **ASSETS** of firms and may be referred to as **CAPITAL ASSETS.**

6.4 **SERVICES** constitute intangible utilities, and may be further sub-divided into **PERSONAL SERVICES** and **COMMERCIAL SERVICES.** Personal services satisfy needs through personal attention such as hairdressing, entertainments or medical treatment. Commercial services are not directly personal but act as aids to production, and include activities such as banking, insurance and communications.

7. The purpose of production is therefore to create utilities by providing a flow of goods and services to fulfil wants. In order to undertake production it is necessary to combine the resources available. These resources are known as the **FACTORS OF PRODUCTION,** and they can be combined in various proportions to produce economic goods. The factors of production can be classified as

7.1 **LAND**
7.2 **LABOUR**
7.3 **CAPITAL**

The activity of combining these factors of production is referred to as **ENTERPRISE**, which is sometimes included as a fourth factor of production. Enterprise is undertaken by the **ENTREPRENEUR** who accepts the **RISK** of producing in advance of sale and in return receives **PROFIT**, the rest of the revenue from sales going in payments to the other factors of production.

8. The problem of society forcing us to make choices is actually the problem of how to allocate existing resources to different uses and how to allocate the resulting goods and services to different members of society. Different societies may have different approaches to resolving these problems, but the problem remains the same everywhere. The three basic problems which all societies are forced to resolve can be expressed as **WHAT, HOW** and **FOR WHOM?**

8.1 **WHAT?** — refers to the problem of which goods should be produced and in what quantities.

8.2 **HOW?** — refers to the method of producing the goods, making the best use of available resources.

8.3 **FOR WHOM?** — refers to the way in which the total output is to be distributed amongst the members of the community.

All economies face the same problems although their approach to solving them may differ.

9. There are basically three alternative approaches a society may adopt in order to solve the problems of What?, How? and For Whom?, the **FREE MARKET,** the **PLANNED** (or **COMMAND**) **ECONOMY,** and the **MIXED ECONOMY** although in reality it is more like a spectrum with differing degrees of mixture between the two extreme forms of a completely free market economy and a totally planned economy, with few examples of the extremes and most being at some intermediate point between the two extremes.

10. In a free market, or private enterprise economy, all the factors of production are owned by private individuals and the decisions of what, how, and for whom, are made unconsciously by the interaction of market forces. We must assume here that consumers are rational and always attempt to maximise the utility they receive from their incomes, and that entrepreneurs are also rational and always attempt to maximise their profits. Given these assumptions, consumers are free to purchase whatever they wish in the market place. This is sometimes expressed as "consumer votes" in the sense that they will spend more of their incomes (votes) on goods they favour. As the demand for these goods increases their prices will rise, making them more profitable, and entrepreneurs seeking greater profit will respond by entering into production of these goods, thereby increasing their supply. Hence more of those goods for which consumers have expressed a preference are produced. Production is therefore said to respond to the 'price signals' which indicates those goods which should be produced, and **CONSUMER SOVEREIGNTY** is said to prevail over the market.

10.1 The technical problem of 'how to produce' is determined by competition between producers which forces each to adopt the least-cost method of production.

10.2 The problem of 'for whom', the problem of distribution, is determined by relative incomes, which in turn are determined by supply and demand in the markets for productive services. If labour is scarce relative to its demand then wages will be higher and a greater proportion of output will go to wage earners; the same is true of owners of land and capital.

10.3 The concept of consumer votes should not be equated with any concept of 'fairness' in the accepted sense; some people have far more 'votes' than others, and if this is seen as a problem then it is one of income distribution not the price mechanism in itself. (See Chapter 20 for more details on this).

We are now in a position to list the main advantages and disadvantages of the three main types of economy.

11.   Advantages of the Free Market Economy

11.1 Because goods are produced in accordance with consumers' preferences then society's resources are also allocated in line with the preferences of consumers.

11.2 Because production responds automatically to the 'price signals' of the market, there is no need for the activities of thousands of manufacturers to be co-ordinated as this happens autonomously.

11.3 Only those goods which are wanted by consumers are produced.

11.4 People are free to spend their money in whichever way they choose.

11.5 The free market economy offers the opportunity for those people with sufficient drive and initiative to enter production and create wealth.

12.   Disadvantages of the Free Market Economy

12.1 Luxury goods for some may be produced before others have the basic necessities of life.

12.2 During periodic recession valuable resources stand idle.

12.3 The free market may not operate efficiently because of the existence of monopolies, and competition may therefore be lacking.

12.4 Essential goods and services may not be provided or at least not be provided in sufficient quantities by the market. Some of these goods are referred to as 'Merit Goods' as they are thought to be so beneficial to society that they should be available to everybody.

Others which are referred to as Pure Public Goods, can only be adequately provided by Government from tax revenue, for example defence.

12.5 The free market does not allow for the 'social costs' of the entrepreneur's activities e.g. pollution of the environment.

13. The **PLANNED** (or **COMMAND**) **ECONOMY** is characterised by the collective ownership of the means of production and hence the price mechanism does not operate. The decisions of What, How and For Whom are made by a Central Planning Body who make their decisions in view of what they perceive as the needs of society.

14. **Advantages of the Command Economy**

14.1 Necessities for everybody will be produced in advance of luxuries.

14.2 Resources need not stand idle during recession.

14.3 Goods can be distributed according to need rather than income.

14.4 Social costs and benefits can be incorporated into the decision making process.

15. **Disadvantages of the Command Economy**

15.1 The problem of co-ordinating thousands of different production decisions in the absence of price signals. For example, the decision to build 5,000 tractors will require the co-ordination of the production of hundreds of thousands of components, and an incorrect decision can hold up the production of the whole 5,000.

15.2 Goods may be produced which consumers do not want, or goods may not be produced in sufficient quantities, the result being shortages of some goods and surpluses of others.

15.3 The lack of personal involvement may result in a lack of incentive.

15.4 The Central Planning Body develops bureaucratic self interest and becomes insensitive to those it is supposed to be serving.

16. **THE MIXED ECONOMY** is characteristic of most modern economies, and whilst leaving much production in private hands it allows for a substantial role for the Government in the production of

certain goods and services, and controls the worst excesses of the market place. To some extent it attempts to gain the better aspects of both the previous systems. Today the concept of the mixed economy is generally accepted by U.K. governments although there may be disagreement over the extent of the Government's role. The Conservative Government, which came to power in 1979, has made attempts to reduce the role of the State in the economy by 'privatising' some sectors of production and reducing the amount of intervention elsewhere.

The advantages and disadvantages are not listed here as they are self-evident from the advantages and disadvantages of the previous two, but we have listed here the main reasons for the involvement of the Government in the mixed economy.

16.1　To provide those essential goods and services which would not be adequately provided by the free market, in particular those referred to as 'merit goods' such as education and health, or pure public goods such as defence.

16.2　Where market failure occurs, i.e. monopoly; in order to protect the interests of the consumer and prevent the worst excesses of monopoly.

16.3　Where production, if left to the market, would be inefficient due to duplication of plant and capacity, or if produced by large private monopolies would lead to excess power over the consumer e.g. electricity production and supply.

16.4　To maintain services which are important both strategically and economically and which may otherwise be in danger of collapse, e.g. Railways, Rolls Royce Aero Engines.

16.5　To regulate the activities of the private entrepreneur to prevent the worst aspects of private production e.g. environmental pollution.

16.6　To regulate the economy in order to maintain the level of demand, employment, balance of payments and inflation. The simultaneous control of each of these variables is difficult and they may in fact conflict, different Governments emphasising the importance of different variables; however most Government involvement in the economy is aimed at the control of one or more of these macro-economic variables.

16.7   As an act of political belief Governments may assume ownership over some areas of the economy. Generally, Labour Governments tend to favour the extension of the role of the State by Nationalisation, whilst Conservative Governments prefer a less interventionist role. Although when threatened with massive job losses through the loss of a firm at the forefront of technological development and a major exporter, in the form of Rolls Royce Aero Engines Division, the Conservative Government took it under the control of the public sector. Nationalisation may therefore be just as likely to occur as a result of economic and political expediency as of political dogma. As mentioned above, the Conservative Government elected to office in 1979 has been more strongly in favour of the private market than other recent Governments and has undertaken the sale of many state assets in order to return them to the control of the private sector, in the belief that they will be operated more efficiently and require less support from the taxpayer.

SELF ASSESSMENT QUESTIONS

1.   Why might 'merit goods' not be provided in sufficient quantities by a free market economy?

2.   Why is the statement "a free market economy is better than a planned economy" by itself a 'value judgement'.

3.   Give an example of a 'social cost' resulting from private production.

4.   Explain why it may be necessary for the government to intervene in the economy.

Chapter 2

PRODUCTION

1. As a starting point for considering the act of producing goods, or **PRODUCTION,** it is useful to sub-divide production into three broad catergories:

1.1 The **EXTRACTIVE** (Primary) Industries, refers to organisations involved in the extraction of basic (primary) materials, and includes industries such as mining, quarrying, farming, forestry and fishing. The outputs of these industries frequently form the raw materials inputs for other industries.

1.2 The **MANUFACTURING** (Secondary) Industries, are involved in the processing of materials or assembling of components to produce goods such as cars, food, chemicals, and engineering equipment.

1.3 The **DISTRIBUTIVE** Industries complete the chain of production by distributing the finished goods through the channels of distribution, through the wholesaler to the retailer and to the final consumer.

These industries however cannot operate effectively without the assistance of another sector of industry:

2. The **SERVICE** Industries. The service industries provide essential aids to those involved in production and include banking and insurance, advertising, general administration, transport and communications.

TABLE 2.1

Changes in employment*,
GB

	Employees 000s			Change 1973-83	
	June 1973	June 1979	June 1983	No. 000s	% per annum
All industries and services	22,180	22,590	20,460	−1720	−0.8
Agriculture, forestry and fishing	420	360	340	−80	−2.1
Mining and quarrying	360	350	310	−50	−1.5
Manufacturing	7,660	7,050	5,370	−2,290	−3.5
Construction	1,340	1,250	970	−370	−3.2
Gas, electricity and water	340	340	320	−20	−0.4
Services industries	12,060	13,240	13,150	+1,090	+0.9

Source: ECONOMIC PROGRESS REPORT 165.

The U.K. economy has large numbers of people employed in each of these categories, table 2.1 showing the size of the labour force in each sector and recent employment trends.

A characteristic of the U.K. economy in recent years has been the relative decline in the importance of manufacturing industry and the growth of the service sector. The manufacturing sector having declined by 13.6% between 1961 and 1981 and the service[1] sector growing by 12% over the same period. Table 2.2 illustrated the percentage change in output for each sector between 1961 and 1981.

TABLE 2.2

INDUSTRY/SERVICE	% of output in each year				
	1961	1966	1971	1976	1981
Agriculture, Forestry & Fishing	4.1	3.3	3.0	2.9	2.3
Mining, Quarrying & N. Sea	3.0	2.1	1.4	2.2	7.3
Manufacturing	37.2	34.0	32.7	28.9	23.6
Construction	6.6	7.0	7.1	7.0	6.4
Gas, Electricity & Water	2.9	3.3	3.3	3.2	3.2
Transport & Communication	8.7	8.6	8.5	8.7	8.0
Distribution	12.5	11.6	11.4	9.6	9.5
Insurance & Banking	3.2	6.0	7.6	8.2	9.1
Professional Services)	16.8	17.5	10.5	12.8	13.5
Misc. Services)			8.1	8.8	9.5
Public Administration	6.0	6.5	7.6	7.6	7.6
Total Services	53.6	50.2	53.4	55.7	57.2
All Industry & Services	100.0	100.0	100.0	100.0	100.0

Source: Social Trends

3.   When we refer to the **FIRM** or **ENTERPRISE** we refer to the unit of ownership or control. A firm may consist of an individual unit or a parent company with several subsidiary firms. An **INDUSTRY** is usually defined according to the physical and technical characteristics of the output produced and consists of all the firms producing these goods.

[1]Insurance, Banking, Professional and Misc. Services.

4. As mentioned in 1.6 the **FACTORS OF PRODUCTION** are essential for production to take place. They can be combined in various proportions, according to their relative prices, in order to achieve the least-cost combination. The least-cost combination will however change over time as factor prices change according to their demand and supply, and also with changes in technology. It is however not only the quantity of a factor of production which is important but also its quality. We will next consider each of these factors more closely.

5. **LAND** in this context is a wider concept than its everyday meaning, and includes all the natural resources available to man which can be utilised for productive purposes and which are provided freely by nature. It therefore includes building land, farming land, minerals, rivers and seas.

The supply of land is of course relatively fixed, the important point in the study of economics however, is that land can be used for different purposes. Land can be transferred between different agricultural uses or from agricultural to building, and will tend to be transferred to that use where it can earn the greatest yield (income). The location of land cannot be changed however and this is particularly important in town centres where land may have a high **SITE VALUE,** no matter how much the demand for such sites increases the supply cannot be increased and such sites may earn what is known as **ECONOMIC RENT** (See Chapter 16).

6. **LABOUR** In order to produce goods the entrepreneur will need to hire the services of labour in return for a wage. As a productive resource both the quality and quantity of labour are important. The quantity of labour will depend upon factors such as the birth rate, average age of the population, total population size and the number of hours worked. Labour quality is an important factor in productivity and this is dependent upon education, training, the possession of appropriate skills, willingness to accept changes in working practices, and the extent to which the labour force is motivated. Also important are its aptitude and intelligence, its willingness to acquire new skills and to adapt to new technology.

7. **CAPITAL** Capital should not be confused with money. Capital is anything which is created, not for its own use but for the purpose of further production. It therefore has the effect of making the process of production less direct.

Capital can be subdivided into two types, working capital and fixed capital. Working capital is used up during the course of production and consists of stocks of raw materials, work in progress, and finished goods. Fixed Capital is not used up in the production process but is retained within the organisation and includes premises, machinery, fixtures and fittings, and vehicles. Another way to consider it is that working capital consists of items acquired for the purpose of re-sale whilst fixed capital consists of items not bought for re-sale but retention within the business. Items of capital are generally referred to as **CAPITAL ASSETS**.

The nation's stock of capital can be sub-divided into Social Capital, Private and Public Sector Industrial Capital and Private Individual Capital. Table 2.3 below identifies these with examples.

TABLE 2.3

CAPITAL STOCK			
PRIVATE INDIVIDUAL CAPITAL	PRIVATE SECTOR INDUSTRIAL CAPITAL	PUBLIC SECTOR INDUSTRIAL CAPITAL	SOCIAL CAPITAL
e.g. Housing stock	e.g. factories, machines, equipment.	e.g. Nationalised Industries	e.g. Schools, hospitals, roads.

Capital goods can only be created by foregoing **CURRENT CONSUMPTION**, i.e. **SAVING**. Current consumption is foregone in order to increase **FUTURE CONSUMPTION**. However merely the act of saving will not create a capital good, the saved resources must be utilised in order to create a **CAPITAL GOOD**.

The creation of a capital good is often illustrated by reference to Robinson Crusoe on his desert island. He catches 5 fish each day by using a line. He decided to spend three days constructing a net. After constructing the net he can now catch 5 fish in one hour and spend the rest of his time growing other foodstuffs and enjoying a more interesting diet. The cost of his net was the 15 fish he did not catch whilst constructing the net. He had to forego present consumption in order to create a capital good which enabled him to have a higher level of future consumption.

8.   During the act of production each year some of the stock of capital is used up, i.e. machines wear out. This is referred to as

DEPRECIATION. The total amount of capital produced each year is referred to as **GROSS INVESTMENT,** and any addition to the stock of capital as **NET INVESTMENT.** Thus the act of just replacing worn out capital will not increase the stock of capital, so there can be gross investment without net investment, but only net investment will increase the productive capacity of the economy.

therefore
GROSS INVESTMENT - DEPRECIATION = NET INVESTMENT

9.   We can usefully illustrate both the problem of scarcity and choice, of which the conflict between current consumption and capital formation is a prime example, by the use of **PRODUCTION POSSIBILITY CURVES (PPC).**

In order to illustrate the concept we will assume that our economy is capable of producing two goods, Good X and Good Y. It has the choice of devoting all its resources to the production of Good X and having none of Good Y, devoting all its resources to Good Y and having none of Good X, or choosing some intermediate point and having some of both. This is illustrated in Diagram 2.1. At point A

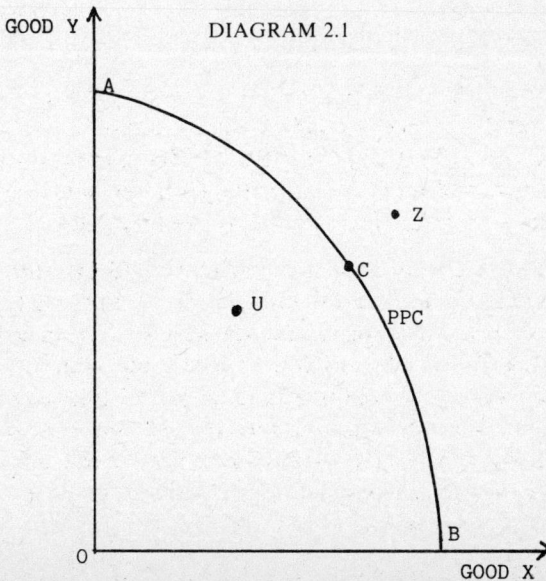

DIAGRAM 2.1

society is producing all Good Y and none of X, and at point B all of X and none of Y. At point C some of both are produced. Note that the shape of the **PPC** is concave to the origin; this is because as we move along the curve from A toward B and factors of production are transferred from the production of one good to the other, as successive units of the factors of production are transferred they will be less and less efficient in their new use due to **DIMINISHING RETURNS**, and for each unit of Y sacrificed we will gain smaller and smaller quantities of X, i.e. the opportunity cost increases. This illustrates that in an economy which is fully utilising its resources **SUBSTITUTION** is inevitable, and wherever there are scarce resources society must always make choices. At point U society's resources are underutilised and we can have more of both goods by moving on to the PPC. Point Z is unobtainable and can only be achieved by a shift of the whole curve upwards and outwards; this can only occur as a result of technological change, increased productivity or an increase in available resources.

DIAGRAM 2.2   DIAGRAM 2.3

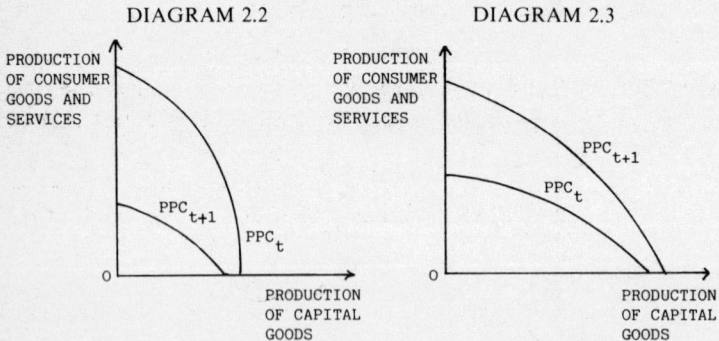

Diagram 2.2 illustrates a society which in the current time period (t) has chosen a high level of consumption and a low level of production of capital goods. In the next time period (t+1) the **PPC** has shifted towards the origin to **PPCt + 1** producing less of both goods and therefore a lower standard of living. Diagram 2.3 illustrates a society which in the current time period has chosen to have a high level of production of capital goods and a relatively lower level of production of consumer goods for current consumption. In the next time period (t+1) however, the **PPC** has shifted outwards to **PPCt+1** and is

enjoying a higher level of consumption and a high level of capital formation — by foregoing some current consumption they enjoyed a higher future 'standard of living'.

10. It cannot be assumed however that because we have more of a factor available we can always gain proportionate increases in output, as inevitably the returns from additional units of factors of production will tend to decline. This is referred to as the **LAW OF DIMINISHING RETURNS** or **DECLINING MARGINAL PRODUCTIVITY**. This states that as we add additional units of a variable factor to a constant factor then the product (output) of the variable factor will first of all rise but will eventually start to decline.

The theory assumes that all the units of the variable factor are identical in terms of productivity, and the techniques of production remain unchanged. In table 2.4 'Total Product' refers to the total output of the variable factor, in this case labour, **Marginal Product** refers to the increase in Total Product from each additional unit of labour, and **Average Product** is

$$\frac{\text{TOTAL PRODUCT}}{\text{QUANTITY OF LABOUR}}$$

In table 2.4 we illustrate the example of a smallholder with one acre of land growing potatoes employing at first a single unit of labour

TABLE 2.4

LABOUR	TOTAL PRODUCT (TONNES)	AVERAGE PRODUCT (AP)	MARGINAL PRODUCT (MP)
1	2	2	
2	10	5	8
3	21	7	11
4	36	9	15
5	55	11	19
6	63	10½	8
7	70	10	7
8	72	9	2
9	72	8	0

and then employing more and more labourers and keeping the amount of land constant. This is represented graphically in diagram 2.4.

As additional labour is added to the fixed factor (land) each successive unit raises output until the fifth man, then the marginal

DIAGRAM 2.4

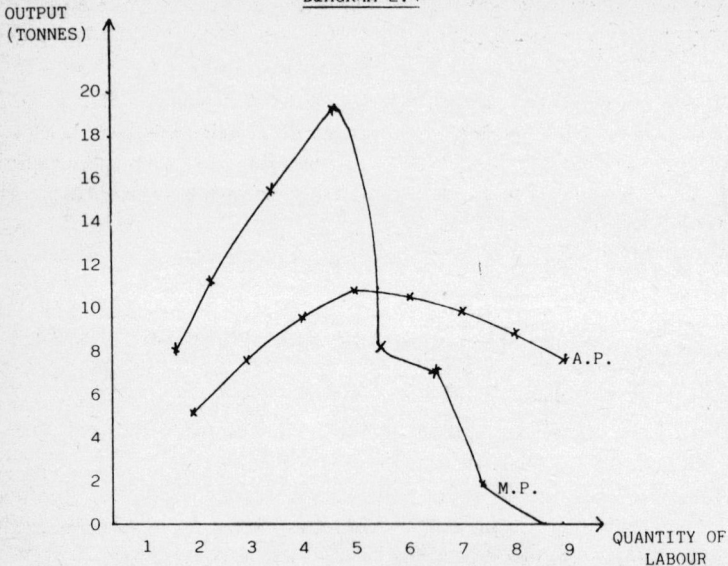

product (MP) begins to decline. Intuitively it can be reasoned that after a certain point each man will have less space to work with and will become less productive. Diagram 2.5 illustrates the behaviour of the **TOTAL PRODUCT. TOTAL PRODUCT** continues to rise but at a declining rate, whilst average product **(AP) and MP** reach a peak at

DIAGRAM 2.5

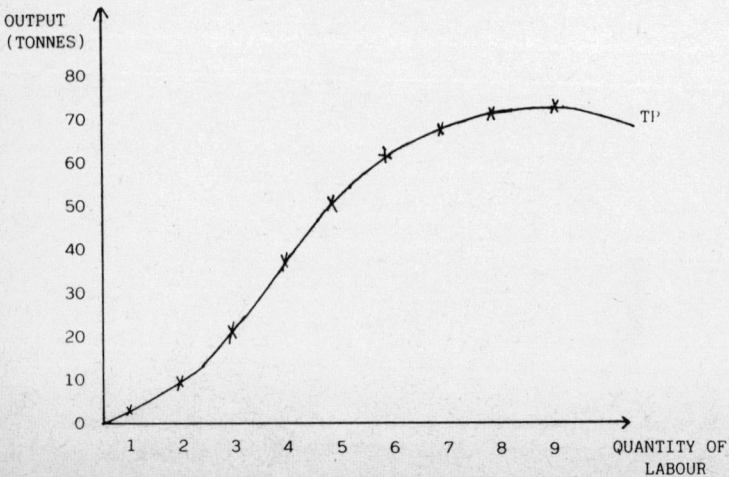

the same number of units. **MP** begins to fall when **THE RATE OF INCREASE** of total product declines. Up to the fifth man total product increases at an **INCREASING RATE** and there are **INCREASING RETURNS**. After the fifth man the **RATE OF GROWTH** of total product declines and **DIMINISHING RETURNS** set in as the marginal product declines. At the point where total product begins to fall, after the ninth man, marginal product becomes negative.

The Law of Declining Marginal Productivity assumes that one factor, in this case land, is held constant. If the amount of land was changed, however, the effect of diminishing returns could be offset. This would represent a change in the **SCALE OF PRODUCTION** and is dealt with later. The Law of Diminishing Returns has important implications for the costs of production and will be referred to again later.

SELF ASSESSMENT QUESTIONS

1. Distinguish between Gross and Net Investment.

2. How is a Capital Good created?

3. What is meant by 'The Law of Diminishing Returns'?

4. Identify the Factors of Production.

5. Why is the Production Possibility Curve concave in shape?

Chapter 3

SPECIALISATION AND THE DIVISION OF LABOUR

1.   In a primitive society where each individual attempts to produce all his own requirements for living, life will be very basic and is referred to as **SUBSISTENCE** living. Output will be very low and each individual will be producing just sufficient to survive. Each individual will be attempting to do his own hunting, fishing, building shelter, farming and making utensils and other requirements. Such production is extremely inefficient as an individual person is unlikely to possess equal talents in each of these activities; he may be good at some and very poor at others. It also means that he must be continually changing from one task to another or leaving some tasks whilst another one is completed.

2.   The single most important element in allowing a society to advance economically is the act of **SPECIALISATION**. Specialisation occurs when each member of a society specialises in that task at which he is most talented. If each individual does this he becomes more productive and total output is increased. The person who is good at hunting devotes all his time to hunting, the person who is skilled at making bows and arrows makes them all the time. Each person now however produces a **SURPLUS** over and above his own requirements, and the essential point is that he can **TRADE** this surplus for those goods which he does not produce.

3.   The gains from specialisation can be achieved even if one person is better at all activities than another, provided one specialises in the activity in which he is most efficient and the other in the acitivty in which he is least inefficient. This is referred to as the principle of **COMPARATIVE ADVANTAGE**. If a person is better at all activities he is said to have an **ABSOLUTE ADVANTAGE** but he may still have a **GREATER COMPARATIVE ADVANTAGE** in the production of some goods and another person will have the **LEAST COMPARATIVE DISADVANTAGE** in the production of others. To illustrate this point, imagine there are two persons, Tom and Dick, both of whom manufacture pans and earthenware pots. Their output per day is as follows:

Tom manufacturers either 40 pans or 40 pots per day.
Dick manufacturers either 37 pans or 16 pots per day.

Prior to specialisation actual output per day is:

Tom manufacturers	20 pans and	20 pots per day
Dick manufactuers	15 pans and	8 pots per day
Total output	35 pans	28 pots per day

Note that Tom is more efficient at producing both but is comparatively more efficient at producing pots, i.e. 40:16, whilst Dick is more efficient at pans, i.e. 40:37. As a result specialisation will raise total output.

After each specialising in the task at which he is most efficient output per day is as follows:

Tom manufactuers	0 pans and	40 pots
Dick manufactuers	37 pans and	0 pans
Total output	37 pans	40 pots per day

Total output has increased by 2 pans and 12 pots per day.

4.   Specialisation is not only the key to how society can raise its output and therefore its standard of living, but is also the precursor of trade.

5.   **Division of labour** refers to the practice of breaking a complex task down into a number of simpler tasks and an individual can then specialise in one of these simple tasks. This is specialisation as most of us know it today in a factory setting where complex tasks, such as building a motor car, are broken down into many thousands of simple tasks, and individual workers specialise in one of them. Specialisation here is a narrower concept with the worker being used where he is most productive rather than most skilled.

6.   A frequently quoted, but nevertheless relevant example, is the observation of a pin factory by the 18th century economist Adam Smith. He noted that the practice of making pins had been broken down into about 18 different operations: one man drawing out the wire, another cutting it, another putting points on, another grinding the heads, another fitting the heads, and so on. The output per head of the factory was about 5,000 pins per day, whereas if each person

had to make the whole pin, Smith estimated that output would have been no more than a few dozen pins per day.

7.   Specialisation and division of labour also occurs with the management functions of a business. As a firm grows it becomes impossible for a single person to have the necessary knowledge of all the functions, and to attempt to perform all of them, all would be extremely inefficient and time consuming. The firm will therefore employ specialists such as accountants, sales managers, engineers, buyers, production managers, and so on.

8.   Once division of labour has taken place and a process has been broken down into a number of simple tasks it becomes easier to apply machines to the tasks. Machines can generally only perform a single task i.e. they are inflexible, however when the process is broken down into its component tasks machines can be applied more easily. This is the way in which **MASS PRODUCTION** is facilitated.

9.   The process of mass production, which carries specialisation and division of labour to its extreme, can be illustrated by reference to one of the earliest examples. Prior to the end of the 18th century muskets had always been individually produced by craftsmen who produced all the components and assembled them. All the

components were unique and would fit only one weapon. At the end of the 18th century Eli Whitney received the contract from the new American Government to produce muskets for the American Army, and was given a year to produce them. Until a few weeks before the delivery was due he had not produced a single weapon; he had in fact been producing the tooling — jigs, dies, stamping machines and setting out the work flow in his workshop. He was then able to produce them within a couple of weeks and fulfil his contract. After that of course he was then able to produce them more quickly and efficiently than anybody else.

Not only did this method produce the muskets more quickly and cheaply, but had a further advantage: all the components would fit any musket as they were identical i.e. they were **INTERCHANGEABLE** or **STANDARDISED,** which meant that assembly was faster, and also that spare parts were available.

This method of production was later developed further by Henry Ford in America, who was the first manufacturer of motor cars to utilise mass production methods with the Model T, which was produced so cheaply and quickly that it became the most popular car in America for nearly 20 years and made the possibility of car ownership a reality for millions of low income Americans.

In recent years mass production has taken a further step forward with the increased use of micro-technology and robotics in assembly processes.

10.   The advantage of specialisation is the productivity gain, which results from the following:

10.1   People rapidly acquire skills when repeatedly performing a simple task.

10.2   Training times and costs are reduced when skills are narrow.

10.3   There is no waiting, or "queuing" time; waiting for machines to become available.

10.4   Time is not wasted moving around the workshop to perform different operations.

10.5   It enables people to perform those tasks at which they have most natural aptitude.

10.6 It facilitates the use of machinery, as machinery is easier to apply to a simple task.

11. There are, however, a number of disadvantages to the process:

11.1 Consistently performing routine tasks soon becomes tedious and boring.

11.2 Specialisation tends to remove the skill from work, hence workers are not given the opportunity to take a 'pride in their work'.

11.3 A combination of 11.1 and 11.2 tends to lead to 'alienation' and as a result poor industrial relations. Workers will tend to lack motivation.

11.4 A narrow specialisation may result in an increased risk of unemployment, and if the whole of the industry is in a recession it may be difficult to find employment. Also skills may become technically obsolete, e.g. cotton mule spinners.

11.5 Where specialisation is taken to extreme, factories themselves tend to specialise e.g. component manufacturers for the car industry. As a result the whole of industry becomes more interdependent, and is vulnerable to a breakdown of any part of the complex chain of production.

12. As mentioned earlier, in 2, specialisation results in surplus production and therefore trade. Early trade takes the form of **BARTER,** where goods are simply 'swapped' for other goods. Barter has a number of weaknesses, however, which make it difficult for an economy to develop.

12.1 Goods are **NON DIVISIBLE** — if a bow is worth $2\frac{1}{2}$ pots, we cannot trade as breaking a pot makes it worthless.

12.2 If we want to trade not only do we need to find somebody who has what we want but he must also want what we have to give in exchange — a **DOUBLE COINCIDENCE OF WANTS.** The possibility of finding such a person is made greater the more people we meet, hence the development of market places where everyone can take their surplus goods and trade. This still happens in many parts of the world.

The weakness of Barter leads to the next vital step in the development of an economy, **MONEY.** Money facilitates the growth of trade and economic development.

13.   Money overcomes the weakness of barter because it has the advantage of being:

13.1   **DIVISIBLE**

13.2   **GENERALLY ACCEPTABLE**

Hence the problems of divisibility and double coincidence of wants are solved. Anybody will accept money and it can be divided into many denominations. Money can in fact be any commodity, and historically cowrie shells, salt, dogs' teeth (New Guinea) and wampum beads (Red Indians), have all been used. The easiest way to ensure general acceptability of a monetary unit is to ensure that it has intrinsic value, hence the popularity of gold coins for so long. We now use paper money which has no intrinsic value, but whose acceptability is based purely on people's confidence. That part of the note issue based on nothing other than people's confidence is known as the **FIDUCIARY ISSUE**. Bank accounts also function as money.

The characteristics needed by a commodity for it to function as money are:

   (i) Generally acceptable
  (ii) Homogeneous (same)
 (iii) Divisible
 (iv) Portable
  (v) Scarce
 (vi) Durable

In this context it is interesting to consider cigarettes, which functioned very efficiently as money in prisoner-of-war camps.

The functions of money can be stated briefly as follows:

   (i) A medium of exchange.
  (ii) A measure of value — the value of goods can be expressed in terms of a standarised unit.
 (iii) A store of value — it is a convenient form in which to store wealth.
 (iv) A method of deferring payments — it facilitates the system of trade credit.

14.   Money has further significance relating to production. The development of money makes wage payments possible; it therefore becomes possible to concentrate the production process into factories where specialisation and division of labour can be carried further, into the system of mass production.

15.   The limits to which specialisation and mass production can be carried are set by:

15.1   The extent of the development of the monetary system.

15.2   The size of the market.

In order to offset the limiting effect of market size countries may join large trading blocks such as the E.E.C., or as in the case of Britain in the 19th century, by trading with an Empire, or by trying to export throughout the world as does Japan today.

16.   Specialisation and division of labour are the pre-requisites for economic development and not surprisingly were described by Adam Smith as "the source of the wealth of nations".

SELF ASSESSMENT QUESTIONS

1. Why does specialisation and division of labour raise output?

2. What are the disadvantages of specialisation and division of labour?

3. Why is Barter inefficient?

4. What are the characteristics of money?

5. What limits the extent of specialisation and division of labour?

Chapter 4
ELEMENTS OF DEMAND

1. We consider next the factors determining market prices. Price, it should be noted, is not the same as value. Value is a subjective evaluation and is not necessarily the same as the price we receive for an item in exchange. We may place a value on an item for a variety of reasons, such as sentiment, but here we are interested only in the value the market places on a good which can conveniently be measured by its price. Market prices are determined by the forces of **DEMAND** and **SUPPLY.**

2. When we refer to **DEMAND** in economics we are referring to **EFFECTIVE DEMAND,** not how much people would like to purchase but how much they can afford and are willing to buy at each price. Demand is, then, the quantity of a good demanded by consumers at a price in a particular time period.

3. At any period of time we can identify a definite relationship between the market prices and the quantity demanded of a good. This can be referred to as a **DEMAND SCHEDULE**. In Table 4.1 we illustrate a demand schedule for potatoes.

TABLE 4.1

DEMAND SCHEDULE FOR POTATOES	
(1) PRICE (£s per tonne)	(2) QUANTITY DEMANDED (000 tonnes per month)
30	25
20	50
15	75
10	125
5	200

Plotting the data in table 4.1 produces the curve illustrated in Diagram 4.1. This is referred to as the **DEMAND CURVE**, identified by the letters DD. From it we can read off the quantities demanded at each price. Note that as the price rises the quantity demand falls and

DIAGRAM 4.1

THE DEMAND CURVE

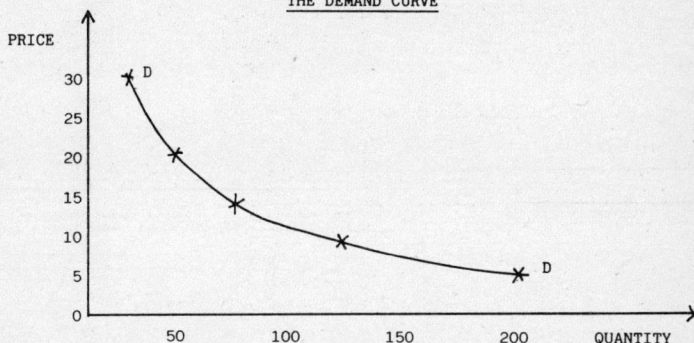

vice versa, the relationship between price and quantity demanded is therefore an **INVERSE RELATIONSHIP**. It is essential to note at this stage that changes in the quantity demanded, or movements along the demand curve occur as a result of **CHANGES IN PRICE ONLY**, all other factors remaining constant, i.e. it is an example of the Ceterus Paribus rule. If other factors do change then there is a shift of the whole demand curve. For example, supposing that there is a substantial increase in incomes so people buy more meat and less potato, this will cause a change in demand in that less will be demanded at each price.

DIAGRAM 4.2

A Movement Along
the Demand Curve

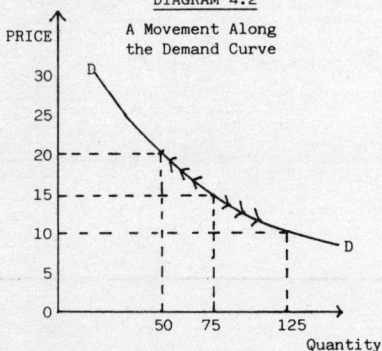

DIAGRAM 4.3

A Shift in the
Demand Curve

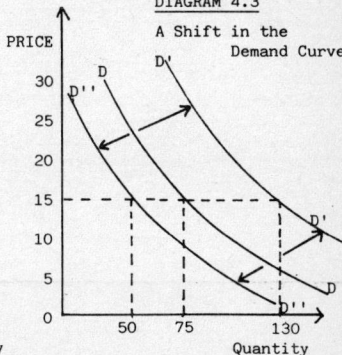

In diagram 4.2 a rise in the price of potatoes causes a movement along the curve, hence the rise in price to £20 reduces the quantity demanded to 50, a fall in the price increases the quantity demanded to 125. Changes in quantity demanded may also be referred to as **EXTENSIONS** or **CONTRACTIONS** in demand.

In diagram 4.3 the **CONDITIONS OF DEMAND** have changed. The change in demand given above, brought about by a fall in the price of meat, is represented in diagram 4.3 by a **SHIFT** of the whole demand curve downwards and to the left, to D"D", and at the price of £15 instead of 75 being demanded, only 50 are demanded. An increase in demand is represented by a **SHIFT** of the whole curve upwards and to the right to D'D' with 130 now being demanded at price 15; the same is true **AT EACH PRICE,** as essentially there is now a new demand curve.

4.   Summary:

   4.1   A change in the **QUANTITY DEMANDED** (or a **CONTRACTION** or **EXTENSION OF DEMAND**) is represented by a **MOVEMENT ALONG THE DEMAND CURVE.**

   4.2   **A CHANGE IN DEMAND** occurs when the change occurs in the conditions of demand and are a result of **FACTORS OTHER THAN PRICE.**

        Changes in demand can occur as a result of
  (i)   Changes in the price of a substitute good (see 7.1).
 (ii)   Changes in the price of a complementary good (see 7.2).
(iii)   Changes in tastes or fashion.
(iv)   A change in incomes.
 (v)   Advertising.

5.   Demand curves are nearly always drawn as sloping downwards from left to right, consequently we refer to the **LAW OF DOWNWARD SLOPING DEMAND.**

Demand curves slope downwards because:
   5.1   As the price of a good falls it becomes available to more people.

   5.2   As the price of a commodity falls it will be substituted for other commodities which have become relatively more expensive (Substitution Effect).

   5.3   As the price of a commodity falls it increases the **REAL INCOME** of the consumer who can then buy more of all goods (Income Effect).

5.4   As we obtain more of a good the utility (satisfaction) we receive from it tends to decline, we will therefore value it less highly and will only be prepared to buy it at a lower price. This is referred to as the Law of **DIMINISHING MARGINAL UTILITY.**

6.   Although there have been many attempts to measure utility it remains a subjective concept. To illustrate the concept, imagine a consumer who had not had a bar of chocolate for many years; if he now received a chocolate bar he would enjoy a high level of satisfaction, or utility, from it and would therefore value it highly in terms of price. If he now received a second bar he would receive more utility but not as much as from the first; his **TOTAL** utility is increasing, but his **MARGINAL** utility is declining, and he will place a lower value on the second and subsequent bars than on the first. Eventually he may feel quite ill from consuming chocolate and place no value at all on further bars. Diagram 4.4 illustrates the marginal utility from each additional bar of chocolate declining whilst total utility increases at a declining rate. In diagram 4.5 the marginal units are plotted separately and the smooth line A-B drawn through them is identical to a demand curve. The concept of Diminishing Marginal Utility underlies the slope of the demand curve and is useful in explaining other aspects of consumer behaviour.

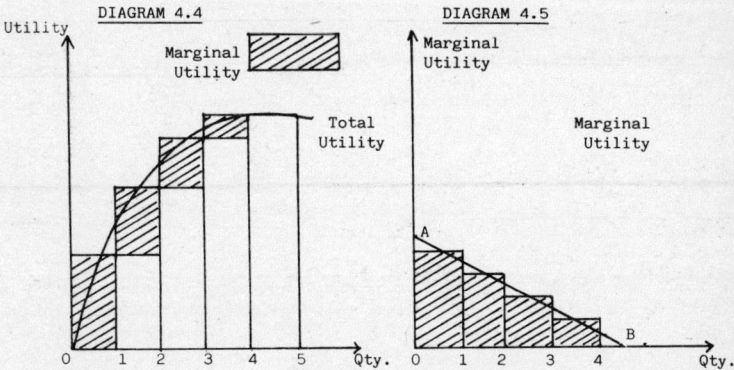

DIAGRAM 4.4

DIAGRAM 4.5

7.   Not all goods are completely independent in demand and the change in the price of one good may affect the demand for other goods.

7.1   **SUBSTITUTE GOODS (COMPETITIVE DEMAND).** An example of a substitute good is margarine and butter. Margarine (the

INFERIOR GOOD) will be substituted for butter (the **NORMAL GOOD**) if the price of butter rises and vice versa if the price of butter falls. When the price of coffee doubled after the crop failure in 1976, there was a substantial increase in the demand for tea.

7.2 **COMPLEMENTARY GOODS (JOINT DEMAND).** These are goods which normally go together such as shoes and laces, cars and tyres, bread and butter.

We can summarise the effect of changes in one of the two goods as follows:

(i) A rise in the price of a good will result in a fall in the demand for that good and an increase in the demand for its substitute. A fall in the price of a good will reduce the demand for its substitute.

(ii) A rise in the price of a good will result in a fall in the demand for that good and therefore a reduction in the demand for its complement. A fall in the price of a good will increase the demand for its complement.

8. There are a few exceptions to the Law of Downward Sloping Demand, which are sometimes referred to as **EXCEPTIONAL DEMAND CURVES** or **REGRESSIVE DEMAND CURVES.**

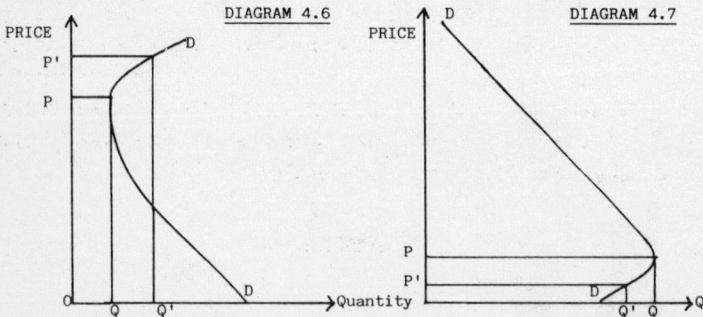

DIAGRAM 4.6   DIAGRAM 4.7

Diagram 4.6 illustrates the case of regression at the upper end of the curve and may occur with **GOODS OF OSTENTATION,** such as jewellery, antiques or paintings. An increase in the price from P to P′ increases the quantity demanded from Q to Q′. People attribute status to such goods and if sold too cheaply people will not feel they are receiving something providing the necessary status. This has certainly been found to be the case with imitation jewellery and it is not uncommon for antiques dealers to find they can sell certain items more easily when the price is raised.

Commodity dealers who take a price increase as an indication of even higher prices in the future will increase the size of their current purchases in the hope of avoiding the highest prices.

Diagram 4.7 indicates regression at the lower end of the curve. A price fall from P to P' reduces the quantity demanded from Q to Q'. This may occur with certain inferior goods, in such cases these goods are referred to as **'GIFFIN GOODS'**. When a high percentage of household income is spent on such goods, any substantial price reduction will increase household income and the additional income will be used to purchase more of the superior good and less will be bought of the inferior good, potatoes and meat being the classic example. It is in fact a case of the Income Effect outweighing the Substitution Effect.

Commodity buyers who take a price fall as an indication of even lower prices in the future will reduce the size of their current purchases hoping to re-enter the market when the price has reached its lowest point.

The vast majority of goods however follow the Law of Downward Sloping Demand.

9. Each consumer has his own individual demand schedule and demand curve for the commodities he purchases, and in order to derive the market or industry demand i.e. the total demand for the output of the commodity, we merely sum horizontally each individual's demand curve at each price.

DIAGRAM 4.8

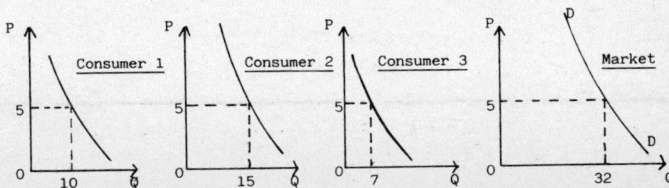

In diagram 4.8 each consumer's demand at Price 5 is added to give one point on the market, or industry, demand curve. This can be done at every price to give a complete market demand curve. Market or industry demand curves always slope downwards because if the industry as a whole increases or lowers price, then the quantity demanded will increase or decrease, but for each individual firm in the industry this may not be the case (see Chapter 10).

SELF ASSESSMENT QUESTIONS

1. What is meant by 'effective demand'?

2. Why do demand curves generally slope downwards?

3. Distinguish between a movement along a demand curve and a shift in the demand curve.

4. Give one example of an exception to the Law of Downward Sloping Demand.

5. What is meant by Diminishing Marginal Utility?

Chapter 5
ELEMENTS OF SUPPLY

1.   Supply refers to the quantity which a producer is willing to put on to the market at a particular price during a particular time period.

2.   Supply is ultimately determined by cost and costs tend to rise as output is increased (see Chapter 8). If we imagine a farmer producing potatoes, if he is to expand output of potatoes he will first of all need to replace other crops, such as barley, with potatoes, which he will only be willing to do if the price of potatoes is sufficiently high to yield him a higher return than the alternative crop. If he wishes to expand output further he may need to utilise marginal land which is not normally used. Such land will require the application of more labour and fertiliser and will therefore be more expensive to cultivate; a higher price will therefore be required by the farmer before the use of such land is considered. The law of supply therefore, says that **MORE OF A GOOD WILL BE SUPPLIED AT A HIGHER PRICE THAN AT A LOWER PRICE.**

3.   In order to illustrate the relationship between price and supply we will utilise the example of the quantity of potatoes a farmer is willing to put on the market at different prices, and table 5.1 is an example of such a **SUPPLY SCHEDULE.**

TABLE 5.1

SUPPLY SCHEDULE FOR POTATOES	
(1)	(2)
PRICE (£s per Tonne)	QUANTITY SUPPLIED (000 Tonnes per Month)
30	150
20	100
15	75
10	50
5	0

4.   By plotting the data we produce the **SUPPLY CURVE** as illustrated in Diagram 5.1, identified by the letters SL. From it we can identify the quantity which will be supplied at each price. As the price

rises the quantity supplied also rises. Note that the curve slopes upwards to the right and we therefore refer to the **LAW OF UPWARDS SLOPING SUPPLY.** Supply curves therefore in general slope upwards and to the right. Like the demand curve, the supply curve is drawn on the ceterus paribus assumption — that no factors other than the price change. If other factors do change then there is a shift of the whole supply curve.

DIAGRAM 5.1

THE SUPPLY CURVE

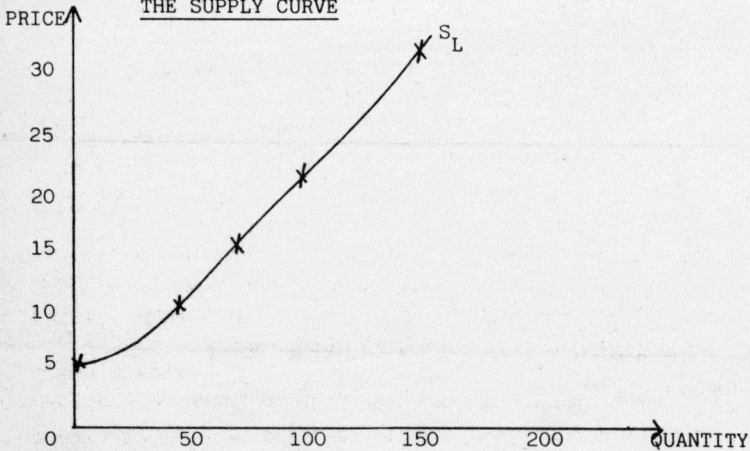

5. Movements along a supply curve occur in response to **PRICE CHANGES ONLY** and are referred to as a change in the **QUANTITY SUPPLIED** (or a **CONTRACTION OR EXTENSION OF SUPPLY**).

6. A **CHANGE IN SUPPLY** occurs when the change occurs in the conditions of supply and are a result of **FACTORS OTHER THAN PRICE.**

Changes in supply can occur as a result of

(i) Technical change i.e. changes in productivity as a result of technical innovation.
(ii) Changes in working practices.
(iii) Weather — important for natural commodities.
(iv) Changes in Taxes or Subsidies.
(v) Changes in the prices of the factors of production affecting costs.

7.

7.1 Diagram 5.2 illustrates the effects of price changes on the quantity supplied, an increase in the price raising the quantity supplied and vice versa.

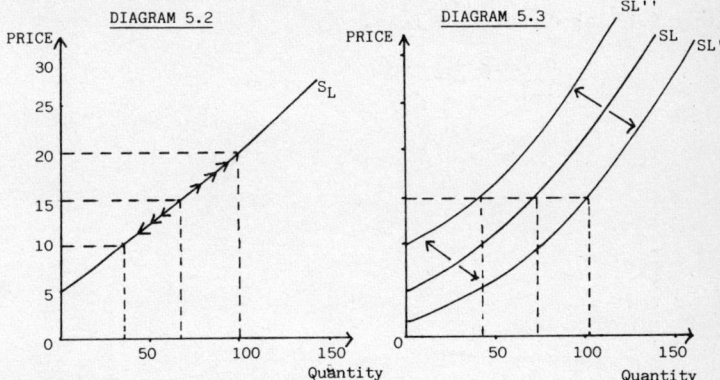

7.2 Diagram 5.3 illustrates a change in supply, resulting from a change in the conditions of supply, represented by a shift in the whole supply curve. An **INCREASE** in supply is represented by a shift of the entire curve downwards to the right from SL to SL', with a greater quantity supplied at each and every price. A **REDUCTION** in supply is represented by a shift of the entire curve upwards to the left, from SL to SL", with a smaller quantity supplied at each price.

8. When some goods are produced it automatically results in the production of other goods, i.e. they are in **JOINT SUPPLY**. For example, an increase in beef production increases the supply of hides. An increase in the supply of petrol increases the supply of all oil derivatives produced in the refining process.

9. One exception to the Law of Upward Sloping Supply is the case of the Backward Sloping Supply Curve for Labour, illustrated in Diagram 5.4. An increase in the wage rate (the price of labour) from W to W' actually reduces the number of hours worked from Q to Q'. The supply curve is normal up to W then slopes backwards. This is because at higher wage rates some labour may prefer to take some of the extra income in the form of time off.

Most goods however follow the Law of Upward Sloping Supply.

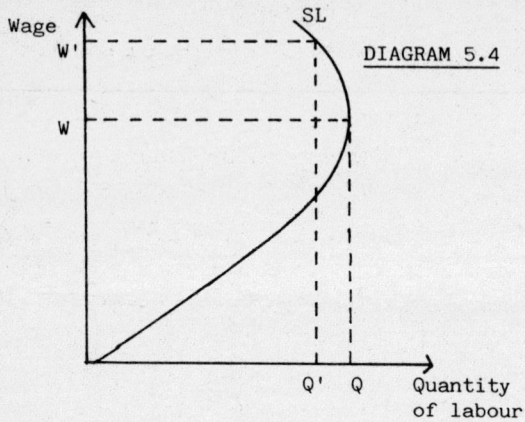

DIAGRAM 5.4

SELF ASSESSMENT QUESTIONS

1. Why do supply curves slope upwards?

2. Distinguish between movements along a supply curve and a shift in the supply curve.

3. What effect would improved machinery have on the supply curve?

4. What effect would the abandonment of a restrictive labour practice have on the supply curve?

Chapter 6

THE DETERMINATION OF MARKET PRICE

1. Having considered both demand and supply, we are now in a position to analyse the way in which market prices are determined.

2. The price of a commodity is determined jointly by the interaction of demand and supply. In order to illustrate this we can now combine the Demand Schedule (Table 4.1) and the Supply Schedule (Table 5.1) in Table 6.1 below.

TABLE 6.1

COMBINED SUPPLY AND DEMAND SCHEDULES FOR POTATOES		
(1) PRICE (£s per tonne)	(2) QUANTITY DEMANDED (000s tonnes per month)	(3) QUANTITY SUPPLIED (000s tonnes per month)
30	25	150
20	50	100
15	75	75
10	125	50
5	200	0

By plotting both the demand and supply curves on to a single graph we can obtain the market price. Market price is that price at which demand and supply are equal, and in Diagram 6.1 can be seen to be the point where demand and supply curves intersect. It is generally

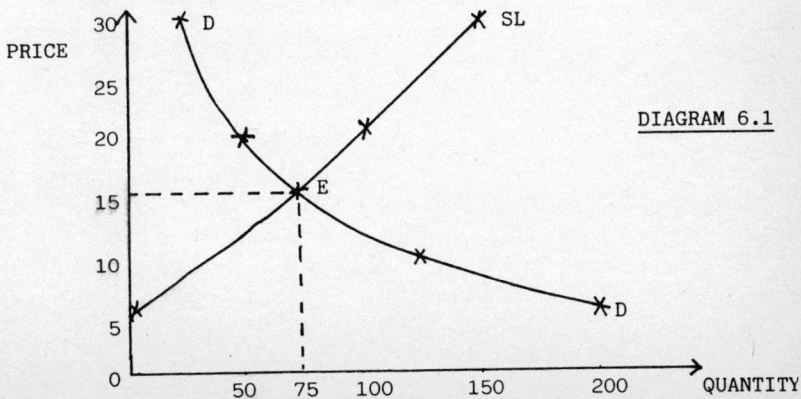

DIAGRAM 6.1

referred to as the **EQUILIBRIUM PRICE (E),** and here the equilibrium price is £15 with quantity 75. This can also be found by inspecting the demand and supply schedules for the price at which demand and supply are equal. At any price below £15 demand will exceed supply and shortages will result; at any price above £15 supply will exceed demand and there are surplus stocks on the market.

3.   For further analysis of equilibrium price we will identify prices by using P and quantity by Q.

Market price, or equilibrium price is therefore the price at which demand and supply are equal. Equilibrium price is the price at which the market will clear i.e. the amount consumers are willing to buy is exactly the same as the amount suppliers will willingly supply: there

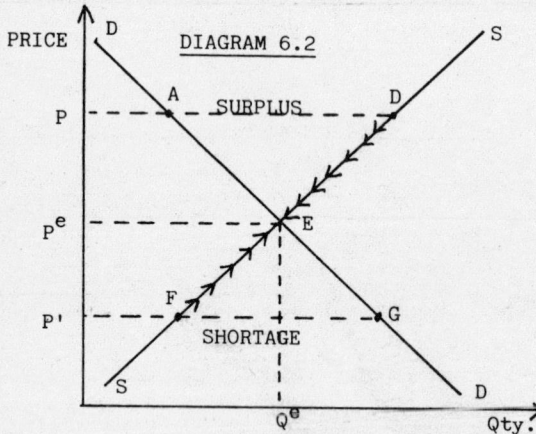

DIAGRAM 6.2

are no shortages and no unsold stocks on the market. In diagram 6.2 demand and supply curves intersect at the equilibrium price Pe and quantity Qe. If at the commencement of the day's trading the price was set at P, there would be an excess of supply over demand and there would be an unsold surplus on the market of A-D. The only way in which these surplus stocks could be cleared would be to reduce the price, which would continue until the market equilibrium (E) was established, with demand and supply equal at price Pe and quantity Qe. If the price was set at P' demand would exceed supply by F-G and a shortage would prevail at that price. The excess demand would bid up prices and producers would respond by increasing supplies, which would continue until market equilibrium was achieved at price Pe and quantity Qe. Equilibrium price is therefore the **PRICE TO WHICH A MARKET WILL ALWAYS RETURN IN THE SHORT RUN.**

This analysis of equilibrium price makes the 'ceterus paribus' assumption that all other factors remain unchanged, however over different time periods other factors may change resulting in different equilibrium prices. It is necessary next to examine more closely how changes in the factors underlying demand and supply may affect market prices.

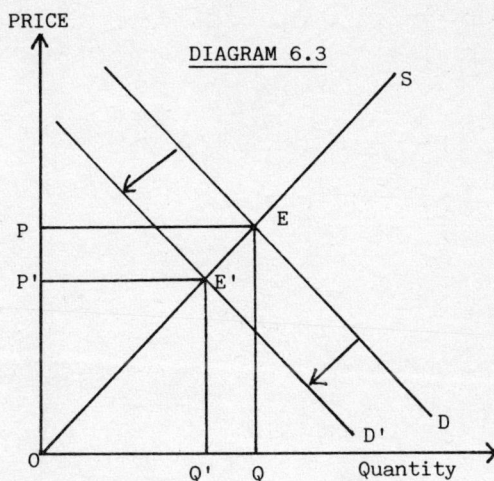

DIAGRAM 6.3

4.

Diagram 6.3 illustrates the market equilibrium for a good, for example butter, at price P and quantity Q. A substantial fall in the price of margarine would increase the demand for margarine and shift the demand curve for butter in the diagram downwards from D to D', with a equilibrium at E', a market price of P', and quantity Q'. Less is now demanded at each price. A rise in the price of margarine would have caused a shift of the demand curve in the opposite direction, there would be an increase in the demand for butter as consumers' preferences switched to the commodity which had become relatively cheaper in order to maximise the utility they receive from their income. Similar shifts in demand can also be as a result of changes in consumers' tastes and preferences, for example if consumers became convinced that consuming too much butter was likely to be a health hazard. A similar shift from D to D' could also be the result of a heavy advertising campaign by the producers of margarine.

5.

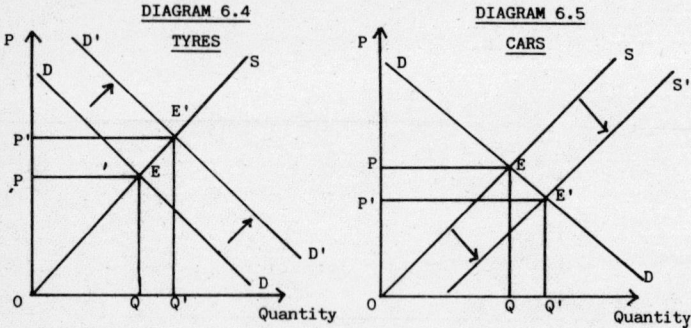

DIAGRAM 6.4
TYRES

DIAGRAM 6.5
CARS

Diagram 6.4 illustrates the market for tyres, and Diagram 6.5 the market for cars, both of which are complementary goods. The car industry now introduces more productive technology such as 'robotics' which lower the costs of production, hence the supply curve shifts from S to S', and there is a movement along the demand curve DD to a new equilibrium at E', with lower price P' and greater quantity Q'. As a result there is a change in the demand for tyres, with the demand curve shifting from DD to D'D', with higher price P' and quantity Q' with equilibrium at E'.

6. Diagram 6.4 above can be referred to as a **PARTIAL EQUILIBRIUM.** If the higher price P' persists for a substantial time period as illustrated in Diagram 6.6., the tyre industry may attract more factors of production and become more productive, shifting the supply curve down to S' with new equilibrium at E" with lower price P". The final equilibrium price may even be lower than P. As the final equilibrium price in the long run after the factors of production have adapted to the new situation cannot be stated with certainty, it is said to be **INDETERMINATE:** whilst the short run position in 6.6 can be stated with certainty and is said to be **DETERMINATE,** which occurs before all factors of production have adjusted to the new market situation.

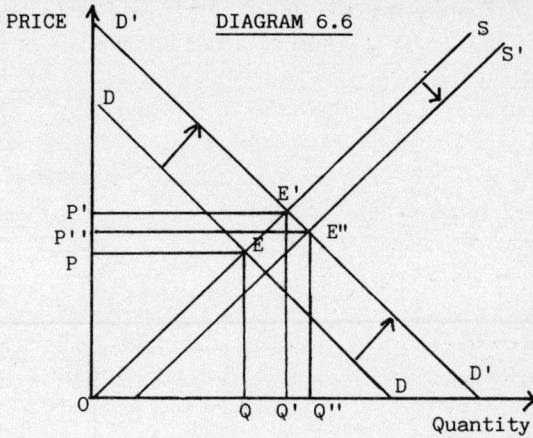

PRICE   D'   DIAGRAM 6.6

7. In this section we consider some applications of demand and supply analysis.

If the Government attempts to control rents and sets a rent ceiling of Rc below the market equilibrium E, then Q° will be demanded and only Q supplied leaving a shortage of rented accommodation of J-K.

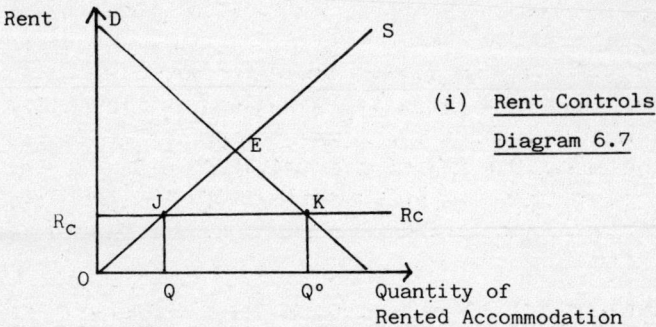

(i) Rent Controls
Diagram 6.7

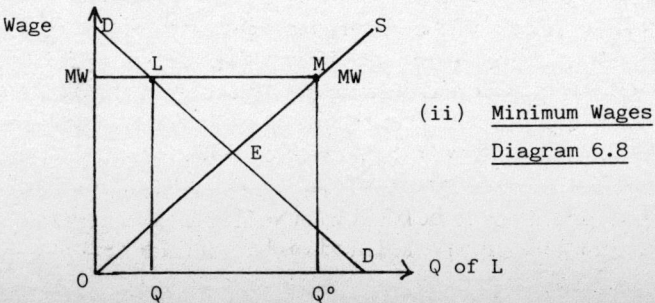

(ii) Minimum Wages
Diagram 6.8

Attempts to force up wage levels by imposing a legal minimum wage, such as MW, results in a surplus of labour (more people wanting jobs than can obtain them at the prevailing wage rate). At MW, Q is demanded and Q° supplied, leaving a shortage of LM. An attempt was made in Costa Rica to raise wage rates in such a way with exactly the results predicted above.

In both cases there would have been no problem if the controls had been set so as to coincide with the market equilibrium price.

(iii) Rationing — Diagram 6.9

(iv) Indirect Tax Incidence — Diagram 6.10

Diagram 6.9 illustrates the attempt by a government to impose rationing. As a result of an increase in demand from D to D′ the equilibrium price rises to E′. The Government attempts to control the price at CP, however at this price there is a shortage of EM. To achieve the ceiling price the Government must reduce 'effective demand' back to DD by some form of rationing such as ration tickets. Even so some of the shortage will still be met illegally on 'black markets' at the market equilibrium price E′.

Incidence refers to who bears the burden of a tax. Diagram 6.10 illustrates the incidence of an indirect tax payable by a producer on each unit of sales. The tax is A-B, and shifts his supply curve upwards by the amount of the tax, but the price to the consumer increases by only P to P′ i.e. C to E′, whilst DC is absorbed by the producer. The amount which is passed on and the amount which is absorbed depends upon the relative demand and supply elasticities (see Chapter 7), in this case 50% each.

SELF ASSESSMENT QUESTIONS

1. What is meant by 'equilibrium price'?

2. How does an increase in the firm's costs (cet. par.) affect equilibrium price?

3. What would be the effect of a legal minimum wage set below the equilibrium wage?

4. Distinguish between partial and full equilibrium.

5. Illustrate by the use of demand and supply diagrams the effect on the equilibrium price of coal of a susbtantial increase in the price of oil.

Chapter 7
ELASTICITY

1. **TOTAL REVENUE (TR)** refers to the firm's total receipts in monetary terms from its sales. It can be calculated therefore as **PRICE × QUANTITY** i.e. $TR = P \times Q$. This is also the area of the rectangle below the demand curve, shown as the shaded area in

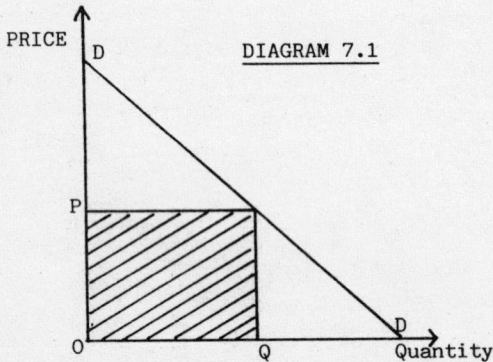

diagram 7.1. The area of this rectangle, and therefore T.R. will change as prices are changed, and of course firms will want this area of T.R. to be as large as possible. **PRICE ELASTICITY OF DEMAND (P.E.D.)** refers to the way in which T.R. changes with variations in price.

2. Intuitively we can reason that a firm may reduce its price and by so doing sell so many extra units that its T.R. is increased, despite charging a slightly lower price per unit. Alternatively a firm may raise its price but in so doing lose so many units of sales that its T.R. declines. In both cases the opposite is also possible, i.e. reducing price may decrease T.R., and in raising price T.R. may increase. This effect on T.R. of a price change is referred to as **PRICE ELASTICITY OF DEMAND (P.E.D.).** A more precise definition is: **PRICE ELASTICITY OF DEMAND IS THE RELATIONSHIP BETWEEN THE PROPORTIONATE (OR PERCENTAGE) CHANGE IN PRICE AND THE PROPORTIONATE (OR PERCENTAGE) CHANGE IN QUANTITY DEMANDED.**

3. Where the quantity demanded is highly responsive to price changes demand is said to be **ELASTIC** and where it is unresponsive it is said to be **INELASTIC**. This can be illustrated by the use of demand curves, however with the exception of three 'special cases' **THE SLOPE OF THE DEMAND CURVE IS NOT NECESSARILY A GUIDE TO ELASTICITY**, and extreme care should be taken in interpreting diagrams.

Diagram 7.2. illustrates the concept of elastic demand. A price reduction from £2.00 to £1.80 increases quantity demanded from 60 to 90, a 10% reduction in price has resulted in a 50% increase in demand, as a result T.R. has increased from £120 to £162. A price increase has the opposite effect and T.R. falls. Demand is very responsive to price changes in both directions.

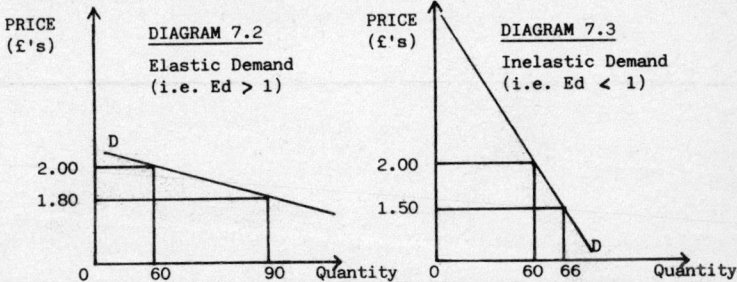

Diagram 7.3 illustrates the concept of inelastic demand. A price reduction from £2.00 to £1.50 increases the quantity demanded from 60 to 66, a 25% price reduction has resulted in an increase in quantity demanded of 10%, as a result T.R. has fallen from £120 to £99. A price increase has the opposite effect and T.R. increases. Demand is unresponsive to price changes in both directions. It is important to realise however that these diagram only represent elasticity within the relevant part of the demand curve and in different parts of the demand curve elasticity will be different (see 7.7 later).

4. Visual comparisons of the elasticity of demand can only be made when the following conditions apply:

4.1 The scales are identical (note that in Diagram 7.2 and 7.3 changing the scale changes the slope of the curve.

4.2 Price changes are identical.

4.3 The price at which the comparison is made is identical.

5. Elasticity of demand, except in three 'limiting cases', varies at different points on the demand curve, and (except in the three special cases) there is no such thing as elastic or inelastic demand curves because measurements of elasticity are relative measures, which depend upon percentage changes taken at a particular point, whilst diagrams represent absolute changes. For this reason it is preferable to measure P.E.D. by the use of formulae.

6. The formula which is most commonly used to measure P.E.D. is

P.E.D. =

PERCENTAGE OR PROPORTIONATE CHANGE IN QUANTITY DEMANDED

PERCENTAGE OR PROPORTIONATE CHANGE IN PRICE

For percentage changes this can be represented in notational form as

$$P.E.D. = \frac{\% \ \Delta Q}{\% \ \Delta P} \quad \text{(where } \Delta = \text{a small change)}$$

The formula can also be represented as follows:

$$PED = \frac{\Delta Dx}{Dx} \bigg/ \frac{\Delta Px}{Px}$$

Where:

ΔDx = the change in the quantity demanded of good x

Dx = the original quantity demanded of good x

ΔPx = the change in the price of good x

Px = the original price of good x.

The formula measures the degree of change in quantity demanded to a small change in price over a small area on a demand curve; and either percentage or proportionate changes can be used.

TABLE 7.1

PRICE (P)	QUANTITY
6	100
5	200
4	300
3	400
2	500
1	600

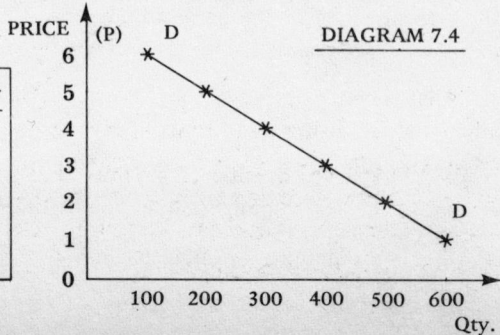

DIAGRAM 7.4

The resulting coefficient gives a measure of the degree of elasticity **around a point** on the demand curve. If it is < 1 demand is inelastic, > 1 demand is elastic, $= 1$ demand is unitary (see diagram 7.8) or 0 demand is totally inelastic (see diagram 7.6).

Table 7.1 is a simple demand schedule and diagram 7.4 is its demand curve.

Using the formula to obtain an estimate of P.E.D. for a price reduction from 5p to 4p we have

$$\text{P.E.D.} = \frac{\% \ \Delta Q}{\% \ \Delta P} = \frac{\dfrac{100}{200} \times 100}{\dfrac{1}{5} \times 100} = \frac{20\%}{50\%} = 2.5$$

which represents a high degree of elasticity.

For a price reduction from 2p to 1p we have

$$= \frac{\dfrac{100}{500} \times 100}{\dfrac{1}{2} \times 100} = \frac{20\%}{50\%} = .4$$

which represents an inelastic demand. This illustrates the fact that P.E.D. varies along a demand curve, and along a straight line demand curve will vary from 0 to ∞ (zero to infinity).

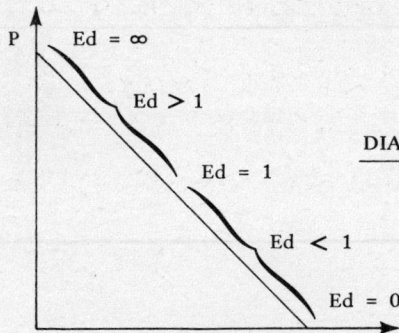

DIAGRAM 7.5

Diagram 7.5 illustrates how a straight line demand curve passes from ∞ through an inelastic portion to the mid-point which is unitary, through an inelastic section to zero at the axis.

(Ed = Elasticity of Demand).

8.   There are three special or 'limiting' cases of P.E.D., referred to earlier, and here the demand curve is a true representation of the P.E.D.

DIAGRAM 7.6   DIAGRAM 7.7   DIAGRAM 7.8

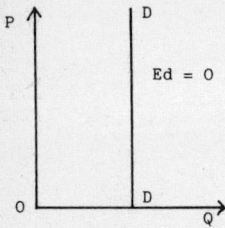
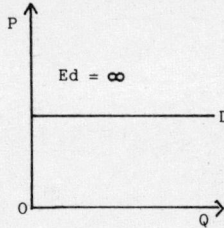
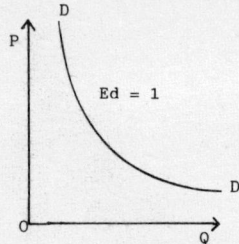

Diagram 7.6 represents the case where Ed = 0, quantity demanded will be totally unresponsive to price (within a relevant price range).

Diagram 7.7 represents the case of the infinitely elastic demand curve Ed = ∞ . Any increase in price will result in zero being demand, any reduction in price will result in an infinitely large demand (this is the perfectly competitive case — see Chapter 10).

Diagram 7.8 represents the unitary demand curve Ed = 1. As price is varied quantity demanded varies proportionately to maintain a constant T.R. Mathematically it is a rectangular hyperbola.

9.   P.E.D. is determined by the following factors:

9.1   The number and closeness of substitutes.

9.2   The proportion of income the good accounts for.

9.3.   Whether the good is a necessity or a luxury.

10.   An estimate of price elasticity of demand is an important element in a firm's pricing policy, particularly when it is considering price increases or reductions.

It is also important for the Chancellor of the Exchequer when selecting goods for the imposition of taxes or duties. It is preferable to select goods which are in inelastic demand in order to be certain of maintaining the tax revenue, e.g. petrol, spirits, beer and cigarettes.

11.   Other measurements of elasticity include

11.1 **INCOME ELASTICITY OF DEMAND (I.E.D.)** which measures the responsive of demand for a good to changes in income. Measured as

I.E.D. =

$$\frac{\text{Percentage change in Quantity Demanded}}{\text{Percentage change in Income}}$$

11.2 **CROSS ELASTICITY OF DEMAND** which measures the responsive of the quantity demanded of one good to the change in the price of another good. Where goods are close substitutes cross elasticity is high. Measured as

Cross Elasticity of Demand for X
with respect to Y

$$= \frac{\text{Percentage change in Quantity Demanded of Good X}}{\text{Percentage change in the price of Good Y}}$$

12. The concept of elasticity also refers to **SUPPLY** and **ELASTICITY OF SUPPLY** can be defined as the **RESPONSIVENESS OF THE QUANTITY SUPPLIED TO CHANGES IN PRICE.**

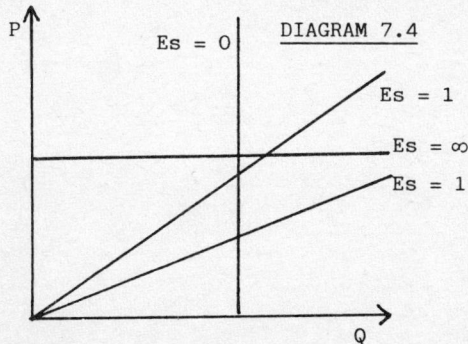

Diagram 7.4 illustrates different supply elasticities. It should be noted that any straight line supply curve passing through the origin is unitary. Elasticity of supply = 0 occurs when supply is fixed and cannot be increased, for example Rembrandt paintings.

13.   The time period involved is very important when discussing elasticity of supply. There are three time periods which are relevant to elasticity of supply; the **MOMENTARY,** the **SHORT RUN** and the **LONG RUN.**

13.1   The momentary period is the period in which no adjustment of either fixed or variable factors of production can occur in response to a change in demand.

13.2   The short run is that period in which variable factors only can adjust to a new situation.

13.3   The long run is that period in which both fixed and variable factors can adjust.

DIAGRAM 7.10

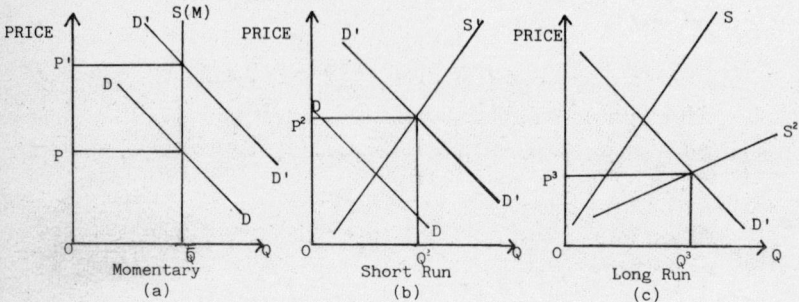

Momentary (a)	Short Run (b)	Long Run (c)

In diagram 7.10 (a) there is an increase in demand from D to D', but in the momentary period supplies are fixed at $\overline{Q}$ and supply is completely inelastic. For example if demand for fresh fruit suddenly increases supplies at Convent Garden cannot be immediately increased. After a period of time has passed supplies can however be increased as variable factors are used more intensively; in this example fruit farmers work longer hours and send more to market. As a result supply becomes more elastic i.e. S' in 7.10 (b), and the price falls to P^2. In the long run both fixed and variable factors have had time to adjust, fruit farmers will have increased their acreage, employed more labour and machines, and new farmers will have entered the industry. Supply has become more elastic, S^2 in diagram 7.10 (c) with the long run price P^3 lower than P^2, with higher demand at Q^3. Whether the long run price P^3 is above or below the original price P depends upon how easily the industry has been able to obtain the additional factors of production it requires for expansion or whether the required factors had to be attracted from alternative uses by paying more for them. Also the extent to which the industry was able to gain economies of scale (see Chapter 8) from its expansion will affect the long run equilibrium price.

SELF ASSESSMENT QUESTIONS

1. Why is the gradient of the demand curve not a reliable indicator of Price Elasticity of Demand?

2. With reference to table 7.1 calculate the Price Elasticity of Demand for a price increase

    (i) from 2p to 3p
    (ii) from 5p to 6p.

3. State the three limiting cases where the demand curve is a guide to elasticity of demand.

4. What are the three time periods relevant to Elasticity of Supply?

5. What factors determine the Price Elasticity of Demand for a commodity?

Chapter 8
THE FIRM'S COSTS

1. During the act of production the firm will incur certain costs and it is necessary to examine how these costs behave as output changes. It is necessary to consider how costs behave with a fixed set of plant and capacity, and also how they behave over the longer period when plant and capacity can be varied.

2. Costs can be classified as either **FIXED COSTS** or **VARIABLE COSTS.**

2.1 **FIXED COSTS.** Fixed costs (sometimes referred to as overhead costs) do not vary with output, they remain constant, or fixed. Examples of fixed costs (F.C.) include rent, rates, interest on loans, depreciation of plant and equipment. No matter to what extent the firm is utilising its capacity this group of costs remains unchanged. This should not be taken to mean that F.C.s never change, for example rates may increase; but they do remain constant over fairly long periods, and more importantly, do not vary with output.

2.2 **VARIABLE COSTS.** Variable costs (VC) are costs which vary directly with output. Examples of variable costs (also referred to as direct costs) may include wages, raw materials and power. When output is zero variable cost will be zero and they rise directly with output.

2.3 **TOTAL COSTS.** Total costs are the sum of fixed and variable costs, i.e.

$$TC = FC + VC$$

When output is zero $TC = FC$ and as output rises TC increases with the increase in VC.

3.

4. In order to analyse the effect of output on costs however, it is necessary to identify costs more closely with units of production i.e. the cost per unit. Total costs need to be converted into **AVERAGE COSTS.** To achieve this all that is required is to divide FC, VC and TC by output (Q). Hence we obtain **AVERAGE FIXED COST**

DIAGRAM 8.1

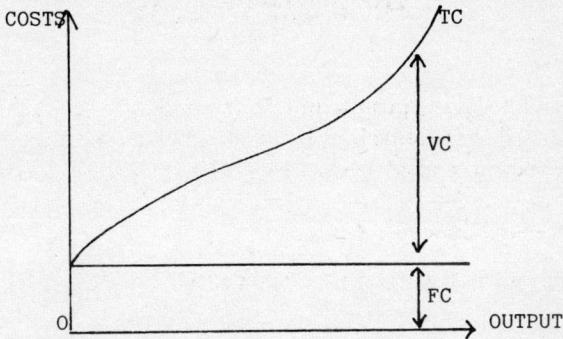

(AFC), AVERAGE VARIABLE COST (AVC) and AVERAGE TOTAL COST (AC).

$$\text{i.e.} \quad AFC = \frac{FC}{Q}$$

$$AVC = \frac{VC}{Q}$$

$$AC = \frac{TC}{Q}$$

Diagram 8.2 represents these average costs diagramatically. Because FC is constant but spread over an increasing number of units it falls over its entire length. AVC falls then rises slowly, whilst AC falls then rises in a U-shaped curve.

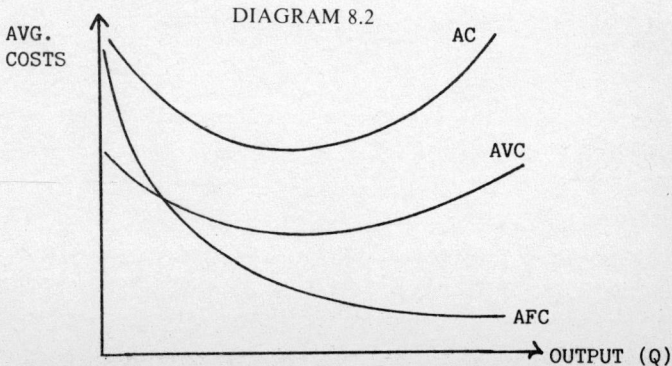

DIAGRAM 8.2

5. The AC is typically a U-shaped curve, with average costs of production falling and then rising. The AC curve falls initially for the following reasons:

5.1 As fixed costs are spread over more units of production the average fixed cost per unit will fall, i.e. fixed costs are £50 and we produce 50 units each unit carries £1 of fixed cost, if output rises to 100 units each unit carries only 50p and so on.

5.2 As more variable factors are added to the fixed factors (land and capital) there will be increasing returns, eventually however diminishing returns will set in, causing costs to rise again. After reaching a minimum the AC curve begins to rise because:

(i) As output increases we may have to employ less efficient labour, as we can assume that the 'best' labour will have been employed first.

(ii) Less efficient machinery may be utilised which would not be used at lower outputs.

(iii) Labour may have to work overtime at higher hourly wage rates.

(iv) Machinery worked consistently at full capacity is liable to more frequent breakdowns.

(v) The managerial problems of co-ordination and control become greater at higher outputs.

The **OPTIMUM** (or ideal) output for the firm is where AC is at a minimum, at the lowest point on the AC curve.

6.   A further essential point about average cost is that in economics **COST INCLUDES NORMAL PROFIT.** Normal profit is that rate of return which is just sufficient to keep the factors of production in their current use and prevent them transferring to any alternative. It can therefore be considered as the **COST** to the entrepreneur of keeping the factors of production in their current use.

7.   **MARGINAL COST** is another very important concept in the study of the firm's costs. Whenever the term 'marginal' is used in economics it refers to the extra, or incremental unit. In the case of costs marginal cost refers to the **ADDITION TO TOTAL COSTS INCURRED BY PRODUCING ONE EXTRA UNIT OF OUTPUT.**

TABLE 8.1

Q	FC	VC	TC	MC
0	30	0	30	15
1	30	15	45	
2	30	25	55	10

8.   Table 8.1 illustrated the concept of marginal cost where it is shown against the mid-points of the increase in output (Q) because it is the increase in costs incurred by increasing output by 1 extra unit. As FC is constant MC is the same as the increase in VC.

TABLE 8.2

Q	FC	VC	TC	AC	MC
0	30	0	30		15
1	30	15	45	45	10
2	30	25	55	27½	5
3	30	30	60	20	10
4	30	40	70	17½	30
5	30	70	100	20	50
6	30	120	150	25	95
7	30	215	245	35	

The derivation of the columns in table 8.2. is straightforward and is explained in 2 and 3. The average and marginal cost data is plotted in diagram 8.3.

Diagram 8.3

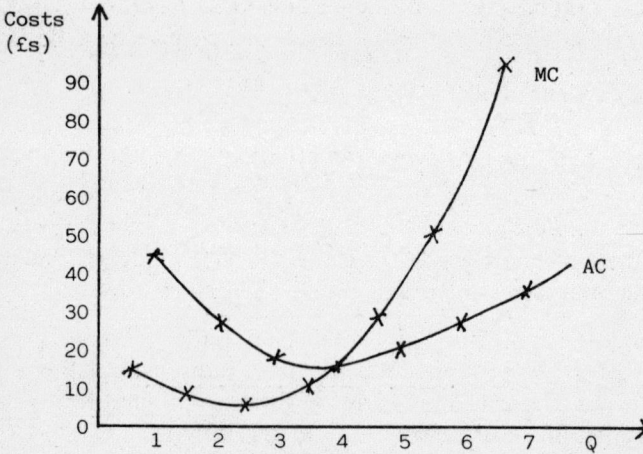

It can be seen that the MC curve falls then rises rapidly **CUTTING THE AC CURVE AT ITS LOWEST POINT.** Whenever MC is below AC, AC is falling and whenever MC is above AC, AC is rising, MC **ALWAYS** cutting AC at its lowest point. This must be the case because of the relationship between MC and AC.

This can be explained by analogy with a darts contest. If a player had scored an average of 100 in ten games and then in his eleventh game scored only 90 then his average would fall to 99. If on the other hand he had scored 110 his average would have risen to 101. It is therefore the additional, or marginal, game which determines the average, and if the marginal score is below the average the average falls, and if the marginal score is above the average, the average rises.

9.   It can be clearly seen from diagram 8.3 that the lowest cost, or optimal output, is at the lowest point on the AC curve, which coincides with the point where MC crosses AC.

10.   All the costs mentioned so far assume that the firm has fixed plant and equipment. It is quite possible however, and indeed

probable, that the firm will vary its plant over the longer period, and as it starts to suffer rising costs may well expand its capacity.

11.   As the firm encounters rising costs it may decide to re-invest and expand its capacity. This new set of plant will have an entirely new AC curve with its optimal output higher than for the previous plant. This is referred to as changing the **SCALE** of production and it is necessary to consider the effect of such changes on **COSTS**.

12.

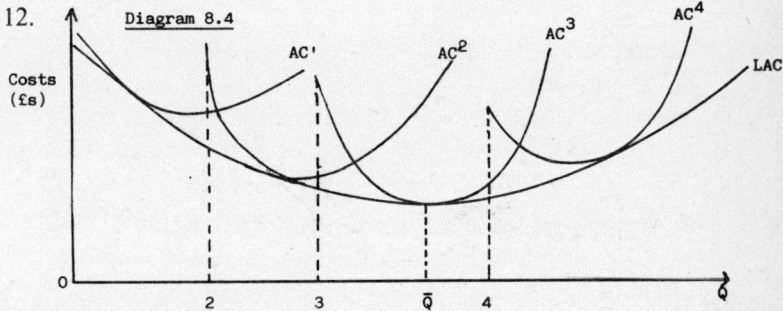

Diagram 8.4

Diagram 8.4 illustrates the effects of changes in the scale of production in long run costs. The firm's first set of plant has AC curve AC^1, but eventually costs rise so the firm invests in a new set of plant which has a greater capacity, with cost curve AC^2, this is repeated for scales 3 and 4, which may represent an overall period of 20 years or longer. Note that when the new plant is introduced i.e. point 2, 3 and 4 its costs may be higher than the minimum point on the old plant, this is because its capacity may not be fully utilised initially, but as ouput grows it moves down its AC to the lowest point.

13.   It should also be noted in diagram 8.4 that minimum point of AC for each successive plant size is lower up to $\overline{Q}$ and then begins to rise again. This is because the **ECONOMIES OF SCALE** resulting from large scale production tend to reduce costs whilst after $\overline{Q}$ **DISECONOMIES OF SCALE** set in and costs start to rise again. $\overline{Q}$ is the optimal long run combination of plant and output but firms rarely recognise when they are at such a point and will more frequently have to attempt to move back to it, after encountering rising costs, by a process of rationalisation.

14. By drawing a smooth curve which touches the lowest point of each short run AC curve as we can derive the **LONG RUN AVERAGE COST CURVE (LAC),** sometimes referred to as the long run **"PLANNING ENVELOPE".** The lowest point on this LAC curve is the long run optimal output $\overline{Q}$.

15. **INTERNAL ECONOMIES OF SCALE** are benefits to the firm which are generated internally and result from larger scale production. They have the effect of reducing the costs of production. Such economies result from:

15.1 **Purchasing Economies:**   Larger firms buy their raw materials and other requirements in larger quantities and in return receive larger discounts from suppliers which contribute to cost reduction. Smaller firms are not able to take advantage of such discounts and therefore pay more for their materials.

15.2 **Marketing Economies:** Larger firms are able to make more effective use of their salesforce. A salesman can negotiate an order for 500 units in almost the same amount of time as one for 100 units. Administrative costs also do not rise in proportion with order size and cost per item ordered are generally much lower. Larger firms are also able to utilise more effective advertising media such as television, and where the product range is wide the advertising of the brand name helps to sell all the firm's products.

15.3 **Managerial Economies:** Large firms can afford, and justify, the employment of specialist managers such as accountants, production managers, sales managers, lawyers etc., whereas in the small firm the managers may have to manage all aspects of the business. The greater degree of specialisation in management leads to greater efficiency.

15.4 **Financial Economies:** Large firms are generally able to raise capital more easily and cheaply than small firms. They have more substantial assets and with a sound trading record, financial institutions see them as representing a lower degree of risk, since they can lay claim to those assets if the firm defaults on payments on a loan.

15.5 **Technical Economies:** Larger firms have greater scope for the division of labour, and specialisation can be carried to a higher degree. This facilitates the introduction of more machinery and specialised equipment which raises productivity. As output increases labour costs per unit of output tend to decline.

15.6 **Indivisibility:** Many production processes are either technically impossible, or not financially viable, on a small scale — they are indivisible in that they cannot be broken down into small scale production. Many chemicals can only be produced commercially on a large scale, the same is true of steel and cars. As firms become larger they are able to take advantage of these more efficient, large scale, manufacturing processes.

15.7 **Risk-bearing** Economies: Larger organisations tend to produce a more diverse range of products; this creates a form of protection in that if one product fails the firm has others which will enable it to survive. Large firms can also afford to undertake high risk activities such as Research and Development into new products. High costs will be incurred during the development stage without any certainty of making an adequate return. When such activity is successful, however, it can be highly profitable, for example the drug industry's expenditure on research is vast but so too are the profits made on a successful new product.

15.8 The **principle of multiplies:** this is a further economy favouring large companies. Machines tend to have different operating speeds and it can be difficult to link them 'end-on' in a production process. This is particularly difficult with only a few machines as it becomes very difficult to ensure a balanced flow which ensures that each machine is being fully utilised. With more machines however larger firms find it easier to organise them in linked processes which ensures that they are all fully utilised.

16. **DISECONOMIES OF SCALE** will set in at some stage in the growth of the firm and result in rising costs. These are more difficult to identify but tend to be more **managerial in nature:**

16.1 As the firm grows the problems of **co-ordination and control** tend to grow rapidly after a certain point and the costs of employing more management (which is not directly productive) grows disproportionately.

16.2 Problems of **communication** arise, both lateral and vertical communications become difficult, not only is it difficult to ensure that instructions are received, but also that they are carried out correctly.

16.3   As organisations grow they may involve production at several separate plants, and the **co-ordination of activities** become less effective.

16.4   Large organisations tend to become more **impersonal,** there is no feeling of 'belonging', hence attitudes of apathy tend to develop, and at worst the workforce becomes 'demotivated' or 'alienated'.

17.   The economies of scale discussed above are all **INTERNAL**, they are generated from within the firm as a consequence of its growth. Another group of economies referred to as **EXTERNAL ECONOMIES OF SCALE** are generated not as a result of the growth of the firm, but as a consequence of the concentration and growth of an **INDUSTRY** within an area. Briefly the major external economies of scale are as a result of:

17.1   A pool of labour with appropriate skills within the area.

17.2   Shared research facilities.

17.3   Appropriate financial facilities.

17.4   The growth of component and other suppliers within the area.

17.5   Appropriate educational course at colleges and universities.

17.6   An appropriate 'infra-structure' developing, i.e. roads, harbours and transport.

SELF ASSESSMENT QUESTIONS

1.   Distinguish between Fixed Costs and Variable Costs.

2.   Why do average costs fall and then rise?

3.   At what point does the marginal cost curve intersect the average cost curve?

4.   In what sense is normal profit a cost?

5.   What is meant by Internal Economies of Scale?

6.   Explain the term Diseconomies of Scale.

7.   What is meant by External Economies of Scale, and why do they occur?

Chapter 9

THE GROWTH OF THE BUSINESS UNIT

1. There appears to be an inevitable tendency for successful organisations to grow in size. The previous chapter indicates that the effect on the firm's costs will be one very important motive for growth, but there are other motives, and in this chapter we analyse what these various motives may be, and the form and direction that this growth may take.

2. The most frequent motives for growth can be identified as:—

2.1 To gain the economies of scale (see Chapter 8).

2.2 To gain dominance over the market by gaining a larger market share i.e. the monopoly motive.

2.3 To diversify into a wider range of products in order to gain greater security e.g. Imperial Tobacco now produce over 60 different products, as diverse as crisps, cigarettes and cardboard cartons.

3. Firms may grow by either internal expansion or externally by merging with, or acquiring, other firms.

4. **INTERNAL EXPANSION** is most likely to occur in an industry which is relatively new and the market is still growing. Growth of this type usually takes the form of expanding the existing amount of plant and manufacturing units. The increase in capacity will enable the firm to:

4.1 Increase the output of its existing products.
4.2 Enter new markets with its existing products.
4.3 Produce a wider range of products.

5. **EXTERNAL GROWTH** refers to growth by means of either **MERGER** or **ACQUISITION**.

5.1 Growth by **MERGER** occurs when two, usually similarly sized firms, decide to join together and merge their separate identities into one.

5.2 Growth by **ACQUISITION** occurs when a business grows by taking over the plants or markets of an existing firm, sometimes referred to as a 'take-over'.

External growth by such methods may make use of a **HOLDING COMPANY**. A holding company is formed specifically for the purpose of gaining a controlling interest (51% of the shares) in a number of other companies. The companies taken over may remain as separate units, but the main policy decisions will be made centrally by the holding company. Examples of holding companies include Charles Forte (Holdings) with interests in Hotels, Catering and Food, the Trafalgar House Group whose interests include insurance and shipbuilding, the Imperial Tobacco Company mentioned above, and Sears (Holdings) Ltd. which has interests in activities as diverse as shipbuilding, footwear, engineering and retailing, and the British American Tobacco Co. whose interests include tobacco and insurance (Eagle Star Insurance). A recent example was the acquisition of the London Brick Company by Hanson Trust.

6. Growth by acquisition or merger is also referred to as **INTEGRATION.** Integration is normally classified according to the direction of the integration, which may be:

  6.1 **HORIZONTAL** — the merging of two firms at the same stage of production.
  6.2 **VERTICAL:**
  (a) **BACKWARDS** towards sources of raw materials.
  (b) **FORWARDS** towards the final market.

7. Horizontal integration occurs when firms engaged in the same stage of production come under a single control. This is very common at the retail stage, for example the merger of Boots and Timothy Whites, and that between Habitat and Mothercare. Some of the UK's largest companies have been formed as a result of such mergers including: United Biscuits, Associated Biscuits, Associated Foods, British Leyland, and GEC. An illustration of a horizontal integration would be the merger of two woollen textile manufacturers. Horizontal mergers may occur in order to gain some of the economies of scale mentioned in Chapter 8. In particular the following economies may be gained:

  7.1 The establishment of a central purchasing department buying the combined requirements of all the companies in the group will gain better discounts for the bulk buying of components and raw materials. Centralised purchasing also facilitates the establishment of better buying and stock control systems, and can employ the expertise of specialist buyers. Large organisations pay considerably less for their supplies than do smaller companies. This is particularly important in retailing where these purchasing economies give a significant advantage to the large retail group over the small independent.

7.2   Financial economies — see Chapter 8.

7.3   Marketing economies — see Chapter 8.

7.4   Technical economies — In addition to the points mentioned in Chapter 8, horizontal integration may create savings in research and development effort. Instead of competing and thereby reproducing costly research effort, research can be centralised, and the pooling of facilities, expertise and effort, can bring considerable savings. Also the combined output of the merged firms may justify the use of larger more efficient machines which would not be fully utilised by the output of a single firm. The same argument can be applied to new technology where robotic production systems and sophisticated computerised control systems can only be justified on the basis of large outputs.

7.5   Managerial Economies — see Chapter 8. Larger firms can afford to employ specialised management, and as there is more scope for division of labour the degree of managerial specialisation can be carried further than in small firms, with the subsequent benefits. Also larger firms can afford to pay the high salaries necessary to attract the most talented managers.

8.   Some significant examples of horizontal integration in manufacturing industry in recent years have been: Allied Breweries and Showerings, GEC and English Electric, British Motor Holdings and Leyland, and the attempted take-over of London Brick by Redland Marley.

9.   Vertical integration refers to mergers which take place between firms who are engaged in different stages of a production process. Forward vertigal integration occurs when a firm merges with a firm at a later stage in the manufacturing process, for example a clothing manufacturer acquiring a chain of retail outlets. Backward vertical integration occurs when the merger takes place with a firm at an earlier stage in the manufacturing process, for example a woollen textile firm acquiring a weaving firm. When the entire manufacturing

process from raw materials to distribution of the finished goods are under the control of a single firm the firm is referred to as 'fully integrated'. At the other extreme where all components are bought out and merely assembled by the firm, the firm is said to be 'disintegrated'. Ford of America is an example of a fully integrated firm. Growth by vertical integration has in the past been a characteristic of the motor car industry as motor car manufacturers attempted to gain control of component suppliers, a typical example being the take-over of the Pressed Steel-Fisher body plant by the then British Motor Corporation. Forward vertical integration in the motor car industry mainly occurs in the form of manufacturers attempting to establish distribution and dealership networks. In the brewing industry it is usually in the form of breweries taking over public houses. In fact the majority of vertical forward integrations are of this type, with manufacturing firms attempting to ensure retail outlets for their products.

10.   Vertical integration may well achieve many of the internal economies of scale mentioned in Chapter 8.15. There may however be additional advantages to be gained.

10.1   Backward integration may be motivated by the desire to ensure the supply of materials which are relatively scarce. This is essentially a defensive motive but it may also be aggressive if these supplies are then denied to competitors.

10.2   Many modern manufacturing processes have very stringent quality control requirements for their components, and attempt to run their production on minimal stocks, they therefore have very tight delivery schedules for supplies. Vertical integration by acquiring component suppliers ensures closer control over the quality of supplies and their conformance with specifications, and also guarantees deliveries. The assurance of quality requirements brings savings in the form of lower inspection costs and lower reject rates during production. Guaranteed delivery performance by suppliers allows firms to reduce their stock levels of components and production materials which reduces their inventory carrying costs; which can be a considerable expense. Many large manufacturers favour such integration as it enables them, with the aid of micro-technology, to introduce techniques such as Materials Requirements Planning, by which supplies are matched exactly with production requirements, resulting in considerable savings in stockholding costs. Such integration has been greatly favoured by the Japanese car and electrical industries.

10.3 The 'end-on' linking of processes is also facilitated by vertical integration, and if this is followed by the concentration of production into a single plant then there may be considerable technical economies. The integration of machines enables machine timings to be set in such a way as to avoid excess stocks of work-in-progress building up, or machines standing idle waiting for another slower part of the process to catch up. Modern steel works such as Ravenscraig provide a good example of integrated production where the production of iron and steel, and the rolling of steel are combined in one continuous process.

10.4 Control over distribution networks is also a source of cost saving. Not only are outlets assured for the firm's products and the costs of distribution reduced, but the firm is also more able to match its production levels to current market demand, particularly where ownership extends to the retail level and market information can be readily fed back to the plant level where sales forecasts and production schedules can be updated in the light of the latest information. This avoids the holding of excess stocks of finished goods or lost sales as a result of shortages. Ownership of distribution channels and retail outlets also enables the firm to eliminate the wholesale function reducing costs and increasing profitability, and also assisting in the marketing and promoting of the product.

10.5 Product diversification may also result from vertical integration. This is the widening of the firm's product range and is a form of protection against the possibility of the failure of a single product putting at risk the survival of the firm. It is in fact one of the economies of scale; that of risk bearing.

10.6 Tube Investments' acquisition of The British Aluminium Company who produced lightweight tubing, is an example of backward vertical integration, and the acquisition, also by Tube Investments, of Raleigh Industries is an example of forward vertical integration. Tube Investments then possessed a tube manufacturer and also a firm which utilised tubing in the manufacture of lightweight bicycles.

11. The majority of mergers in recent years have been of the horizontal type. These have been mainly defensive in character in

order to consolidate market shares in the face of world recession and growing international competition. Despite this the opportunities to gain economies of scale remain one of the main motives for both types of merger, but are still only a single element in a complex decision.

TABLE 9.1

	1965–73	1978	1979
Horizontal (%)	78	53	7
Vertical (%)	5	13	7
Conglomerate (%)	17	34	42

Source: Annual Reports of the Director General of Fair Trading

12. **CONGLOMERATE** mergers are mergers which are not strictly lateral or vertical but are between companies producing a product (or range of products) which are not directly related. The objective may be to reduce risk by diversifying or to enter a new market when the existing market offers little hope for further growth. They are frequently associated with **MULTI NATIONAL COMPANIES** and **HOLDING COMPANIES**. Examples are the Imperial Tobacco Group and Sears (Holdings) Ltd., mentioned above, and British American Tobacco which acquired Eagle Star Insurance, and Hanson Trust's acquisition of the London Brick Co.

13. Despite the fact that economies of scale appear to offer substantial benefits to large firms many industries are still characterised by the survival of small firms. It is necessary to consider therefore why small firms survive and why they are so prevalent in some industries, and also why in some industries both large and small firms exist alongside each other. The main reasons are outlined below.

13.1 Where personal attention is involved and growth of the firm would involve loss of personal attention to detail. Examples are hairdressing and bespoke tailoring.

13.2 Where the total market is small, output will not be sufficient to achieve the necessary levels of specialisation and division of labour. Examples include retailing in isolated communities where only 'general' shops can survive because the limited demand prohibits specialised retailing. Garages tend to be small because the market is limited by the distance people are willing to travel for car repairs, and also the nature of the work does not lend itself the achievement of economies of scale.

13.3   Some industries provide highly individualistic or 'exclusive' items. Such items are generally luxury goods and if produced on a large scale would lose their attraction as their appeal is their uniqueness. Such goods will frequently be the creations of talented individuals and as the supply of such people is limited, the firm is unlikely to grow to large scale. Examples include designing, architecture and high fashion.

13.4   Small firms may survive in an industry by locating a specialised segment of the market which does not interest the large manufacturer who prefers longer production 'runs'.

13.5   In the engineering industry many small firms survive by taking work which is sub-contracted to them by larger firms who have no spare capacity and have too much work, or where the small firm provides a specialised service to the larger firms. Small firms may also undertake the highly specialised 'one-off' jobs that are of no interest to the larger firms.

13.6   Large firms may allow small firms to exist in order to prevent investigation by the Monopolies Commission (see Chapter 13).

13.7   The fact that a firm is small may merely be due to the fact that it is in an early stage of its growth and is one of the large firms of tomorrow.

14.   Economies of scale undoubtedly give advantages to larger firms, but there is little doubt that there will always be a place for the small enterprising firm, and it may be the case that such firms offer the greatest prospects for economic growth.

SELF ASSESSMENT QUESTIONS

1. What are the two main methods by which firms grow?

2. Distinguish between Vertical and Horizontal Integration.

3. What is meant by Internal Economies of Scale?

4. What are the main motives for Horizontal Integration?

5. Give four examples of Internal Economies of Scale.

Chapter 10
PERFECT COMPETITION

1.   We consider next the various market forms, the first of which is **PERFECT COMPETITION**. In reality very few markets are perfectly competitive, examples being the Chicago Grain Market, the Stock Exchange, and some of the commodity markets; however the concept does provide a yardstick by which the degree of competition in real world markets can be measured. It is assumed here that firms compete on price alone and not the other forms of competition, such as advertising, which may be a charateristic of other market forms.

2.   In order for a market to be considered as perfectly competitive a number of conditions must be satisfied, these are:

2.1   There must be a single homogeneous (same) product i.e. each seller is offering an identical product.

2.2   There must be many buyers and sellers none of whom can alone influence the market price.

2.3   All buyers and sellers must have perfect information regarding the market.

2.4   Perfect mobility of factors of production to and from the industry. If profits are high entrepreneurs can enter the industry, or leave if greater returns can be earned elsewhere.

Given these conditions there can only be a single market price which cannot be influenced by the activities of any single buyer or seller. As competition is based purely on price, and the product is homogeneous, buyers will buy from whoever is the cheapest; therefore each producer is forced to adopt the least-cost method of production and all excess profits or losses will in the long run be eliminated by entry to, or exit from, the industry.

3.   We can illustrate the concept by using a simple diagram (diagram 10.1). In diagram 10.1 we have a buyer in a market place where there are six sellers all selling an identical product, say for example bags of sugar. The buyer knows the price each seller is charging and we assume that the buyer behaves in a rational manner. Assume that seller 1 raises his price while the others all keep theirs

constant, clearly the buyer will buy zero from seller 1 and obtain his requirements from the others. On the other hand if seller 1 reduced his price whilst the others kept theirs constant, the others would all sell zero and seller 1 would sell all that the buyer was willing to take. This is in fact another way of saying that the firm in perfect competition has an **INFINITELY ELASTIC DEMAND CURVE** (see Chapter 7).

DIAGRAM 10.1

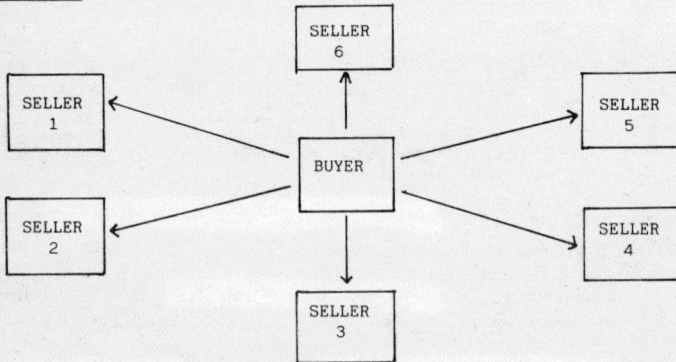

4.   **MARGINAL REVENUE (MR)** is the addition to Total Revenue which a firm receives from the sale of one extra unit of output.

AVERAGE REVENUE (AR) is the same as price. This is obvious if we consider that Total Revenue is defined as PRICE x QUANTITY.

$$\text{i.e. TR} = P \times Q$$

$$\textit{therefore } AR = \frac{TR}{Q} = P$$

if AR = P then the **AVERAGE REVENUE** curve is the **SAME THING AS THE DEMAND CURVE.**

5.   In perfect competition as each unit is sold at the same price then both **MR** and **AR** are constant and are the **SAME AS THE DEMAND CURVE**, as illustrated in Diagram 10.2, i.e. **P = AR = Dd = MR.** (See Appendix 1 on page 76.

DIAGRAM 10.2
The Firm

Dd=AR=MR

DIAGRAM 10.3
The Industry

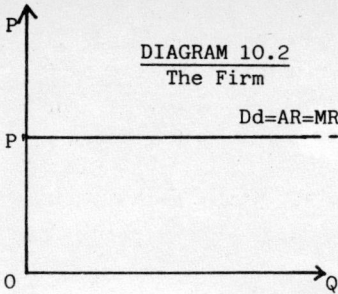

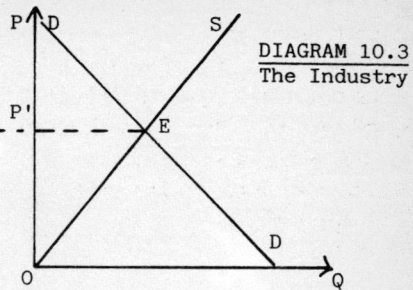

The demand curve, as stated above, is infinitely elastic because if an individual firm raises its price, it will sell all its output at the prevailing market price. The price, in this case P′ in diagram 10.2, is determined by the market and cannot be influenced by the individual firm whose output is too small relative to the total industry output to be able to influence it. The firm in perfect competition is therefore said to be a 'PRICE TAKER' rather than a 'price maker'.

6.   The market price, which applies to each firm, is determined by the market demand and supply curves for the **INDUSTRY AS A WHOLE**. The industry demand curve slopes downwards because if the industry as a whole reduces its price it will sell more. The industry or market equilibrium price, P′ in diagram 10.3, is at the point where the market demand and supply curves intersect. This establishes the price for every firm in the industry. Should the market price fall or rise for any reason then this new price will then apply to every firm in the industry.

7.   It is now possible to derive the competitive firm's **PROFIT MAXIMISING OUTPUT**. The competitive firm's Average Cost (AC) curve is the usual U-shaped curve, and is of course defined so as to include **NORMAL PROFIT**. The MC falls and then rises sharply cutting **AC** at its lowest point. In order to maximise its profits the competitive firm will expand output to the point where **MR = MC**, at point E, in diagram 10.4. This is the competitive firm's equilibrium point with the profit maximising output at Qe. At lower outputs the firm is not maximising its profits, for example at output Q^2 MR exceeds MC by A-B and the firm can increase its profits by the shaded area by raising its output to Qe. At higher outputs than Qe the firm can increase its profits by reducing output, for example at output Q′

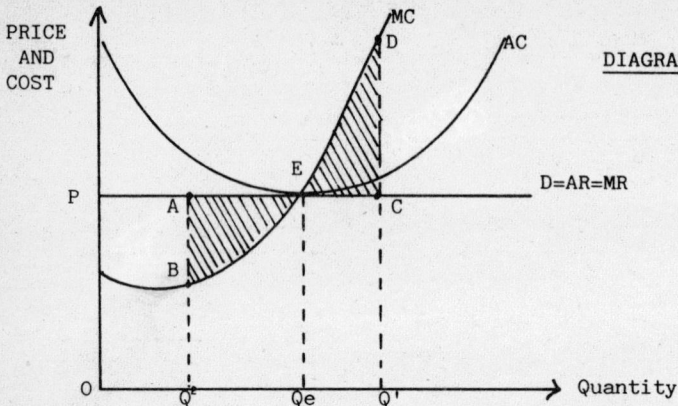

DIAGRAM 10.4

MC exceeds MR by D-C and the firm is therefore making a loss on each additional unit. Profit will therefore be increased by the shaded area if output is reduced to Qe. As the price is just equal to MC at the lowest point of AC, the firm is using its plant at peak efficiency, and is just covering its costs with no abnormal or super-normal profits being earned, only normal profits being made.

The two essential rules to remember are:

7.1   That a firm's profit maximising output is where

$$\boxed{MR = MC}$$

and this is true of firms under **any** market conditions.

7.2   Under conditions of perfect competition the firm's price is equal to the marginal cost.

$$\boxed{P = MC}$$

8.   **SUPER NORMAL PROFITS (SNP)** are profits earned under **CONDITIONS OF PERFECT COMPETITION IN THE SHORT RUN,** during the period of time which it takes for factors of production to enter the industry.

9.   We can now analyse the process by which super normal profits, or losses, will be eliminated in a perfectly competitive industry.

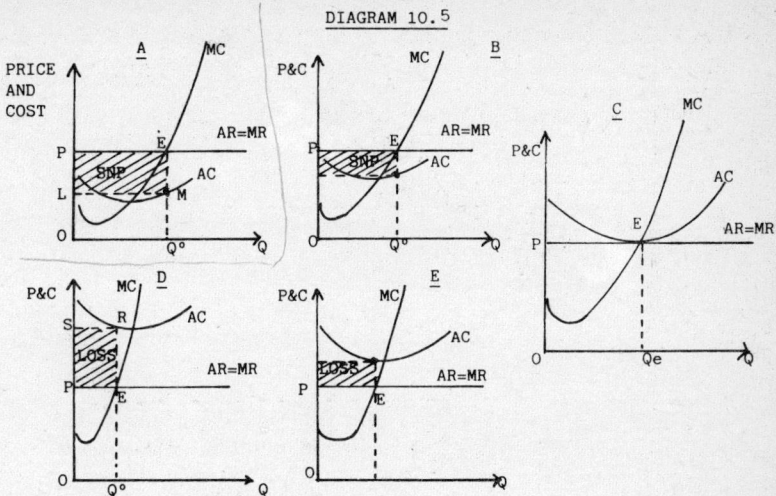

DIAGRAM 10.5

In diagram 10.5 A. the firm has an equilibrium output of $Q°$ (MR = MC at E), and cost is only OL ($Q°M$) per unit, hence the firm is making a super normal profit of PLME. These high profits will attract new entrants to the industry and supply will increase, prices will start to fall and the amount of super normal profit will decline as in B, however as long as SNP is being earned entry to the industry will continue until all SNP's have been eliminated and all firms are earning only normal profits, as in C.

In diagram 10.5 D. the firm has an equilibrium output of $Q°$ (MR = MC at E), but the cost per unit is OS ($Q°R$) and the firm is making a loss of PERS, as is each firm in the industry. Firms will leave the industry in search of higher profits elsewhere, supply will fall and prices rise, reducing the size of the loss, as in diagram E. As long as losses persist firms will leave the industry until eventually each firm which remains is a marginal firm making only normal profit, as in Diagram 10.5 C.

In the long run all excess profits and losses are eliminated and each firm is a marginal firm selling at P = MC.

A recent example of excess profits being eliminated by competition is the Rubic's Cube where entry to the industry by new firms brought the price down from £5 to £1 in less than a year. The same sort of competition is emerging with micro-computers where competition is reducing prices and profit margins rapidly.

10.   Although normal profit applies throughout an industry it is not necessarily the same between different industries. Normal profit can differ between industries due to:

10.1   The degree of risk and uncertainty involved. High risk industries require high profits in order to attract capital.

10.2   The nature of the production process involved. Capital intensive industries require higher rates of return in order to make investment worthwhile.

10.3   Exceptional entrepreneurial ability enables some industries to earn higher profits by skilful management; sometimes referred to as 'rent of ability'.

10.4   There may be quite substantial time lags before firms can enter an industry due to the shortage of skilled labour or the need to construct plant. Such temporary profits are referred to as **QUASI RENTS**, and they occur whenever profits are earned as a result of a temporarily fixed supply of factors of production.

11.   Where firms have specific assets, in the sense that they cannot immediately be used to produce something else if the price of a

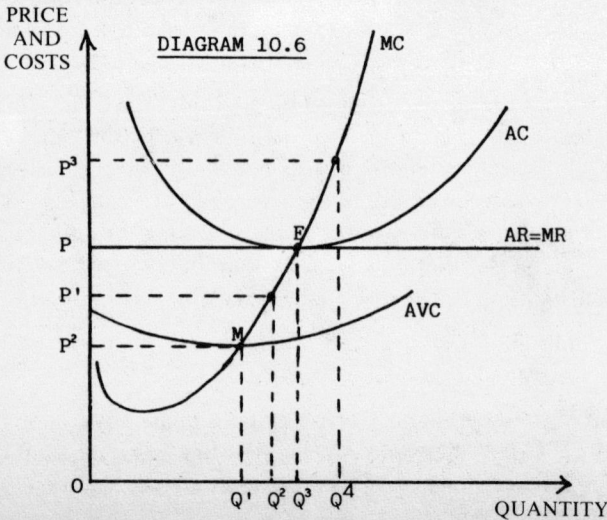

DIAGRAM 10.6

product falls, they may in fact stay in an industry for a period even if the price falls below average cost. In diagram 10.6 the firm is in equilibrium at E with price P and quantity Q^3. If the price falls to P′ the firm will move down the MC curve to the new equilibrium of MC = MR and produce Q^2. The firm will continue to produce until price falls to P^2 at which point it will cease production. Equilibrium point M is therefore referred to as the 'shutdown point'. The firm will therefore continue to produce at any price which covers its average variable costs of production, because anything over AVC makes a contribution to the fixed costs which have to be paid whether the firm produces or not, and will therefore reduce the size of its losses. However if the price falls below its AVC by producing the firm will actually increase its losses, and the more it produces the greater the loss will be. In the short run therefore a firm with specific assets will remain in production as long as the price is greater than AVC.

12.   If we consider the firm's MC curve in diagram 10.6 it can be observed that the portion of it above M relates the price to the quantity the firm will produce, it is therefore the firm's supply curve. **THE COMPETITIVE FIRM'S M.C. CURVE ABOVE AVC IS ITS SUPPLY CURVE.** If the MC curves of all the firms in the industry are summed together we obtain the industry supply curve.

13.   We consider next conditions of **IMPERFECT COMPETITION.** The breakdown of perfect competition occurs when one firm introduces a cost saving innovation and is therefore able to produce more cheaply than its competitors. However, not only does it make the innovation, but it is able to keep information regarding the details to itself and permanently undercut its competitors.

SELF ASSESSMENT QUESTIONS

1.   What are the conditions necessary for the existence of a perfectly competitive market?

2.   At what point will the perfectly competitive firm be in equilibrium?

3.   Where will the perfectly competitive firm in equilibrium set its price?

4. What is meant by Normal Profit?

5. How are Super Normal Profits eliminated from a competitive industry?

6. Describe the relationship between MC and supply.

APPENDIX 1

P	Q	TR	$AR(\frac{TR}{Q})$	MR (Increase in Total Revenue)
5	1	5	5	5
5	2	10	5	5
5	3	15	5	5
5	4	20	5	5
5	5	25	5	5
5	6	30	5	5

As price is constant under conditions of perfect competition P = AR = Dd = MR.

APPENDIX 2

The firms' profit maximising output can also be determined by the use of **TOTAL CONCEPTS**. Diagram 10.7 illustrates **TOTAL COST (TC)** and **TOTAL REVENUE (TR).** The profit maximising output will be at the point where the difference between TR and TC is the greatest, which coincides with the maximum point on the **TOTAL PROFIT CURVE (TP).** This profit maximising output is the same as that obtained in the lower section of the diagram by following the **MR = MC** rule i.e. OQ. This can be proved by drawing parallel lines at a tangent to TC and TR and these lines will be tangential (touching) TC and TR at the profit maximising output. At this point therefore the rate of change of TR and TC are equal i.e.

$$\frac{dTR}{dQ} = \frac{dTC}{dQ}$$

and as $\dfrac{dTR}{dQ} = MR$ and $\dfrac{dTC}{dQ} = MC,$

then at that output **MR = MC**.(note this proof is not essential for A level students).

DIAGRAM 10.7

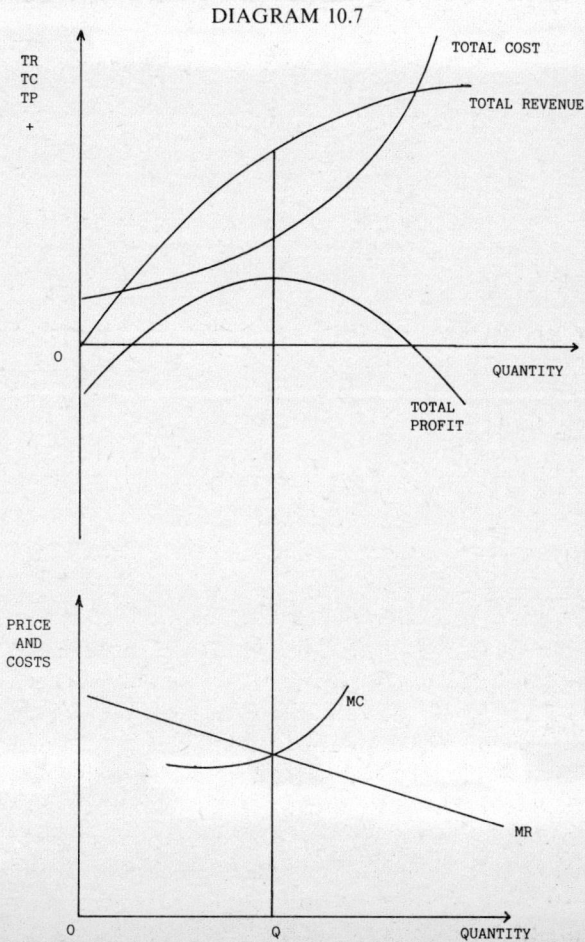

Chapter 11
MONOPOLY

1. Monopoly refers to a market where supply is under the control of a single supplier. In the case of perfect monopoly, this will be a single firm, however the effect will be similar if several firms act together in fixing prices, which is referred to as a **CARTEL**. In both cases the buyer is facing a **SINGLE SOURCE OF SUPPLY**.

2. As the monopolist is the sole source of supply in a market, his demand curve is also the industry demand curve; the monopolist therefore faces a **DOWNWARD SLOPING DEMAND CURVE**. If the monopolist wants to sell more he must reduce the price.

3. Diagram 11.1 illustrates the downward sloping demand curve of the monopolist. It also illustrates another important difference between the monopolist and the competitive firm; the monopolist's

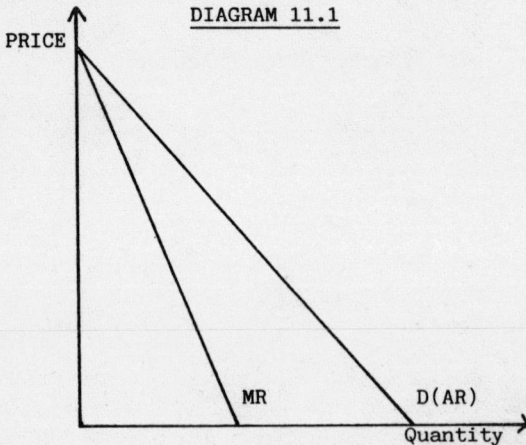

DIAGRAM 11.1

PRICE

MR   D(AR)

Quantity

Average Revenue (AR) is **NOT** the same as Marginal Revenue (MR). MR is in fact **LESS THAN AR**. This is because when the monopolist wants to sell more he must reduce the price, not only on the extra units he sells but also on all of the earlier units. To illustrate assume that a monopolist is selling 10 units at £1 each, therefore TR = £10. In order to increase his sales to 11 units he must reduce the price to .99p each, and TR = 10.89 i.e. 11 × .99. The increase in Total Revenue

(MR) from the sale of the extra unit was 89p, despite the price being 99p. This is because of the 1p cost lost on each of the 10 units sold previously. Mathematically MR has twice the slope of AR (see appendix).

4. The monopolist, like any other firm, finds its profit maximising output where MR = MC, at point E in diagram 11.2, giving output $O\overline{Q}$. Price is however set above the marginal cost of production at M, the appropriate point on the monopolist's demand curve. At output $O\overline{Q}$ however, the average cost of production is only N, producing a **MONOPOLY PROFIT** (or **MONOPOLY RENT**) of PCNM. Unlike the super normal profits earned under perfect competition these monopoly profits will **PERSIST INTO THE LONG RUN** and will not be eliminated by entry to the industry.

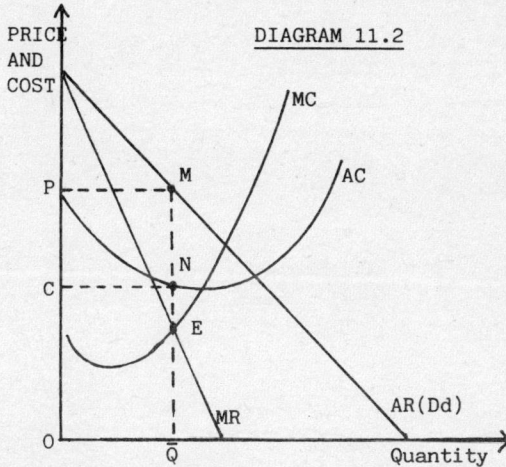

DIAGRAM 11.2

5. From diagram 11.2 it can also be seen that the monopolist, unlike the competitive firm, is not operating at the lowest point on his AC curve, and could in fact be producing more at a lower cost, but he does not choose to do so. Instead the monopolist restricts output and sets price above the marginal cost of production. The monopolist's resources could be used more efficiently elsewhere, hence society's resources are being misallocated. The two arguments against monopoly are therefore:

5.1 They exploit the consumer by setting a price greater than MC.

5.2   They create a loss of efficiency by misallocating society's resources.

It is these two points which frequently lead Governments to take action in order to control or curb monopoly power.

6.   It is sometimes argued that a lump sum tax should be levied upon monopolists equivalent to their monopoly profit which could then be redistributed (i.e. PCNM in diagram 11.2), this would leave their profit maximising equilibrium point E unchanged, and therefore their output. This suggestion however does not overcome the chief objection to monopoly — that of resource misallocation, as the monopolist would still not be operating at the most efficient point on his AC curve.

7.   Marginal revenue is related to elasticity. Whenever MR is positive demand is elastic, and whenever MR is negative i.e. below price P in diagram 11.3, demand is inelastic. A monopolist therefore will never produce at a price where demand is inelastic, because his MR is negative and he can increase his Total Revenue by reducing output.

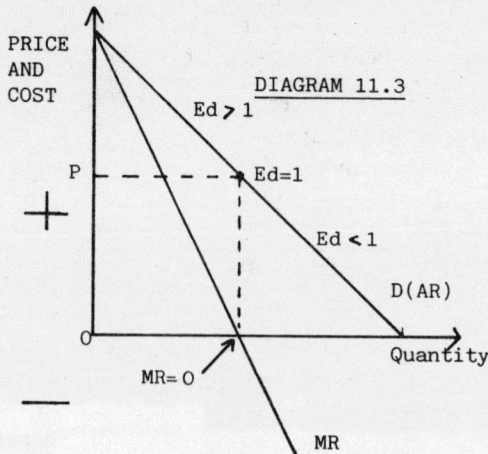

DIAGRAM 11.3

8.   The monopolist's power will depend upon two factors:

8.1   The availibility of substitutes. The greater the absence of substitutes, the greater the power of the monopolist to make profits i.e. the more inelastic is demand over the **ENTIRE RANGE.**

8.2   The ease with which the monopolist can erect **BARRIERS TO ENTRY**, to prevent new firms entering the industry (see Chapter 12).

9.   The monopolist's power however does not extend to the control of demand. Because he cannot control demand he has two options:

9.1   He can control supply and let demand determine price.

9.2   He can set the price and let demand determine the quantity supplied.

He cannot however do both without controlling demand.

10.   The monopolist can make greater profits if he can practice **PRICE DISCRIMINATION**. Price discrimination refers to the charging of different prices in different markets. Price discrimination will be successful under the following conditions:

10.1   There must be no 'leakages' between two markets, i.e. consumers must not be able to travel between markets in order to buy in the cheapest, or buy in one market and re-sell in another. The **SEGMENTATION** of markets may be by either:

(a)   Time. Usually used in the case of non-storable services, for example peak and off-peak rail fares.

(b)   Geographical dispersion. Where markets are widely dispersed geographically, price discrimination can be practised as long as the price differential is less than the cost of transport between two markets, e.g. the price differential between B.L. cars in the U.K. and Germany was pushed to the point where it became cheaper for U.K. buyers to import them from Germany.

10.2   Where the elasticity of demand is different in two markets then charging different prices, a high price in the inelastic market and a lower price in the elastic market, will maximise revenue.

Price discrimination does not only occur under monopoly however, but also under other forms of imperfect competition.

11.   The classical case against monopoly rests upon the assumption they they misallocate society's resources. The analysis so far, however, has been conducted in static terms, which assumes that other factors, such as costs, remain unchanged when an industry is

monopolised. This may not however be the case and monopolisation may generate dynamic changes which produce benefits to society which outweigh the allocative costs.

12. Diagram 11.4 illustrates the monopolisation of a perfectly competitive industry. Original competitive market demand and

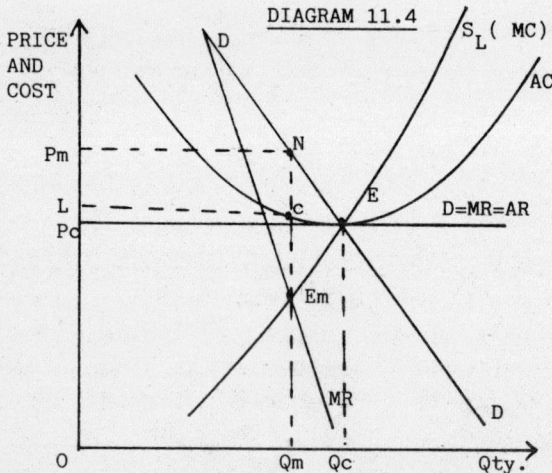

DIAGRAM 11.4

supply curves give equilibrium at E at the bottom of each firm's AC curve, with output Qc. After monopolisation of the industry the industry demand curve becomes the monopolising firm's demand curve with MR lying below it. Equilibrium of MR = MC is now at Em with output Qm, with price Pm and monopoly profit PmLCN. Output is lower and price higher after the industry has been monopolised.

This analysis however assumes that the cost structures remain unchanged, whereas in reality they may well change. The concentration of the production of many small competitive firms may produce such substantial economies of scale that costs will fall as a result.

In diagram 11.5 the competitive industry output is Q with price P. Monopolisation could be expected to reduce output to Q_1 and raise price to P_1. If however monopolisation results in substantial economies of scale which shift costs down from MC to MCm, then the monopolist's output will be higher at Q_2 with the price lower that the competitive price at P_2 despite the existence of monopoly profits.

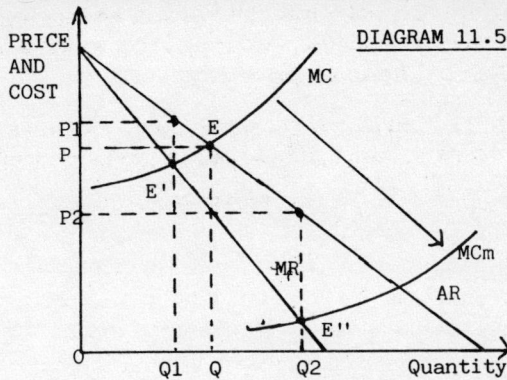

DIAGRAM 11.5

13. Whether monopoly is 'good' or 'bad' must also depend to some extent upon how the monopolist actually behaves and what he does with his monopoly profits. It is quite possible that the monopolist shares his profits with his workforce in the form of higher than average wage rates and working conditions.

14. Monopoly profits may also be reinvested within the firm in the form of research and development. An example of this is the drug industry where substantial profits are made, but at the same time the level of research and development into new drugs is high, and most new drugs are in fact introduced by firms with a high degree of market power. Monopoly also avoids the duplication of research and development effort making more efficient use of resources and more rapid technological advancement.

15. Some authorities such as Joseph Schumpeter and J.K. Galbraith suggest that technical innovation is closely linked to market form and that monopoly is most likely to create the atmosphere which is conducive to innovation. Only monopoly provides the stability in the market which will encourage firms to undertake innovation which is both risky and costly. Only firms making monopoly profits have the resources to undertake extensive research and development, and this will only be undertaken if firms can be certain of achieving a high rate of return on their investment, which would by no means be certain in a competitive environment. Monopoly provides the stability and the returns necessary for such expenditures to be undertaken.

16. Joseph Schumpeter refers to the process of 'creative destruction' in which monopolies make innovations only to eventually have their profits destroyed by competitive activity as the monopolist's profits attract others to try to obtain some for themselves. The classical example of this being the ball point pen which was introduced by the Reynolds Company in 1946, who held a monopoly position at that time. The original price was $12.50 and cost 80¢ to make; however by 1948 competition had entered the industry and the price fell to 39¢ and cost 10¢ to produce, with very little profit left in their production. Patents will not prevent this process as they will be by-passed by the development of similar but slightly different products. Schumpeter estimated that losses due to resource misallocation amounted to no more than 2-3% of national income which was more than outweighed by the increased economic growth generated by innovation.

17. It is therefore by no means certain that in all cases monopoly is harmful, and even accepting the harmful effects upon resource allocation these allocative costs may be outweighed by benefits of the types described above, a possibility which is reflected in U.K. legislative controls over monopoly and mergers (see Chapter 14).

SELF ASSESSMENT QUESTIONS

1. Why is the monopolist's MR less than AR?

2. What are the two main arguments against monopoly?

3. State the conditions which make price discrimination possible.

4. Outline the arguments in favour of monopoly.

5. What factors will determine the market power of a monopolist?

APPENDIX

Proof that for the monopolist the Marginal Revenue Curve (MR) has twice the slope of the Average Revenue Curve (AR). Recalling that **AR = Dd = P.**

The equation for a downward sloping demand curve, or AR curve is:

(1) $P = a - bq$

where
    a = a constant
    b = the gradient of the curve
    q = quantity demanded.

Total Revenue (TR), which is $P \times q$, is obtained therefore by multiplying (1) through by q.

(2) $TR = aq - bq^2$

Marginal Revenue refers to a small change in Total Revenue, so by differentiating Total Revenue with respect to quantity we obtain Marginal Revenue.

(3) $MR = \dfrac{dTR}{dq} = a - 2bq$

therefore
MR has twice the slope of AR (the coefficient for the gradient is 2b rather than b).

Chapter 12
OLIGOPOLY

1.   Oligopoly refers to markets which are **dominated by a few sellers**. The entire output of the industry is produced by a few large firms and the contribution of each firm is sufficiently large to be significant in the market. Oligopoly is the prevalent market form in many areas of manufacturing in Europe and the U.K. The tendency towards oligopoly is a result of the attempts by firms to gain economies of scale by amalgamation and merger. In the U.K. oligopoly is the characteristic market form in the detergents, car, chemicals and oil industries.

2.   Oligopoly is not only distinguished from other market forms by the number of firms but also by a qualitative difference. When the number of competitors in the market are few each seller becomes acutely aware of how his rivals are likely to react to any change he may make, particularly on price. Oligopoly is the only market form therefore where the firm's pricing and output decisions will also incorporate the perceived, or expected, reactions of competitors. Firms are therefore to a certain extent interdependent, the policies of one influencing the other.

3.   This interdependence helps us to understand one of the major characteristics of oligopoly markets — that of **PRICE RIGIDITY**. The prices charged by monopolists tend to be similar even if there is no collusion (i.e. price fixing). It is necessary therefore to analyse the nature of oligopolistic markets and attempt to identify why it is that the prices charged by the different firms tend to be similar even in the absence of a formal agreement.

4.   One explanation for this is the 'Kinked Demand Curve'. This solution suggests that firms in oligopoly potentially face two demand curves, one for price increases which is highly **ELASTIC** and one for price reductions which is highly **INELASTIC**. In diagram 12.1 for price increases the firm is on the elastic curve dd and for reductions it is on the inelastic curve DD, and the firm's actual demand curve is dED; the demand curve has a 'kink' at E with price $\overline{P}$ and quantity $\overline{Q}$, all the firms in the industry being in a similar position. This is because if one firm raises its price and its competitor fails to follow suit then a

PRICE

D

DIAGRAM 12.1

d

E

$\overline{P}$

d

D

O

$\overline{Q}$

Quantity

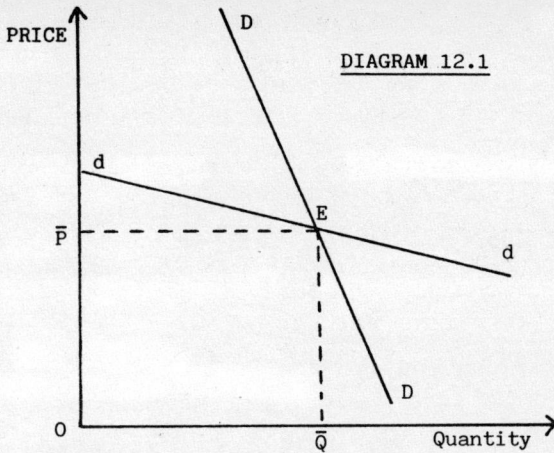

large proportion of sales and therefore revenue will be lost, it is therefore on the elastic position of the curve dE. If one firm attempts to reduce price by itself its competitors have no alternative but to follow suit, and reduce price by at least as much and possibly more in order to retain their market share. Price is now lower but with the same market share, hence the firm is on the inelastic portion of the curve ED. Price reductions may even start a price war which may be disastrous for one firm, a possibility all will want to avoid making any reduction below $\overline{P}$ unlikely. The actual demand curve is therefore dED with prices tending to be inflexible, or rigid, around the 'kink' in the curve at E. This is one explanation of why prices tend to be inflexible in oligopolistic markets, and once firms find themselves in this situation it becomes easier to enter more formal agreements on price fixing.

Such collusion reduces still further the risk of a price war, and in addition to price fixing may involve production quotas or other methods of reducing competition. These methods are however subject to legal controls (see Chapter 14).

In such oligopoly situations a **PRICE LEADER** may emerge. The price leader is accepted informally by all those within the industry as the firm which gives the lead in price increases. When the price leader raises his price the others take it as the signal to raise their own prices to the same level.

5.   Even where substantial cost differences exist between two firms this may not be reflected in market prices. The 'kink' in the demand curve at E in diagram 12.2 produces a vertical section or 'discontinuity' in the marginal revenue curve of both firms, indicated by the letters G-F. Irrespective of where the firms' cost curves intersect this vertical section of the marginal revenue curve price and output will remain unchanged. In diagram 12.2 there is a low cost producer with cost curves AC' and MC' and a high cost producer with cost curves AC and MC, despite the cost differences the price for both remains $\overline{P}$ with output $\overline{Q}$. The weakness of this analysis is that it explains **HOW** the kink in the demand curve occurs but cannot predict **WHERE** it will occur and may therefore be considered as an 'ex post' rationalisation.

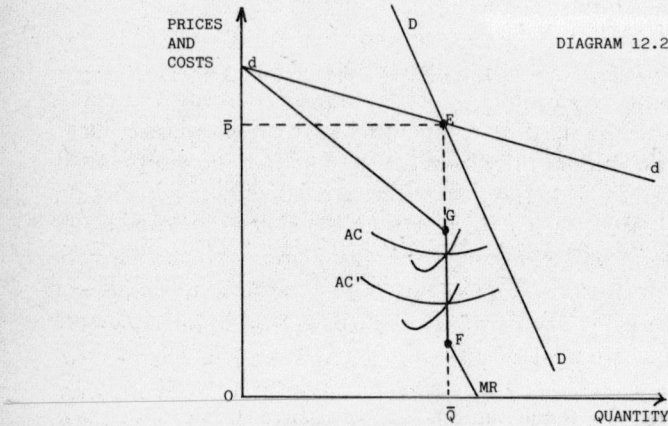

DIAGRAM 12.2

6.   Although firms in markets which are oligopolistic may not compete on price such markets may have the appearance of being highly competitive due to the prevalence of **NON-PRICE COMPETITION.** This non-price competition will occur because although the firms may not wish to compete on price they will still desire to increase their market share and hence their profitability. Firms will not compete on price but competition takes a variety of alternative forms.

7.   Non-price competition may involve some, or all of the following methods:

7.1 There is usually a high level of competitive advertising. Advertising is used to emphasise minor real, or spurious, differences between products, a process referred to as **PRODUCT DIFFERENTIATION**; and also in the attempt to establish brand loyalty.

7.2 'Free' gifts.

7.3 Competitions.

7.4 Coupons which can be collected and exchanged for gifts.

7.5 Special offers.

7.6 Guarantees and warranties.

7.7 Sponsorship.

7.8 After sales service.

An important point is that the consumer may prefer a lower price but is not given that alternative.

8. Monopoly power, whether pure monopoly or oligopoly, will depend in the long run upon how effectively potential entrants to the industry can be kept out. Measures to keep new entrants out of an industry are referred to as **BARRIERS TO ENTRY**. The most commonly found barriers to entry are as follows:

8.1 **EXTENSIVE ADVERTISING** by existing firms in order to create brand loyalty and the high level of product differentiation in the form of branded goods makes entry by new firms difficult. Initially they would at least have to match the advertising expenditure of the existing firms but on the basis of a much smaller market share.

8.2 The **MINIMUM EFFICIENT SCALE (M.E.S.)** of production may be high relative to the market share of the new entrant. A high M.E.S. may be due to the technical economies of scale, where for example production on a small scale is possible only at a very high cost, which on the basis of the small market share which a new entrant would have would be impossible to sustain. Where the M.E.S. is low, advertising may be used as a way of increasing costs, making entry more difficult. Also where existing firms have substantial economies of scale of the type mentioned earlier, the new entrant with a small market share will be at a considerable cost disadvantage. In addition existing firms may adopt

PRICE
AND
COST

DIAGRAM 12.3

AC
New
Entrant

Pe

Pn

PL

MC

AC
Existing
Firm

D(AR)

O

Q

R

Quantity

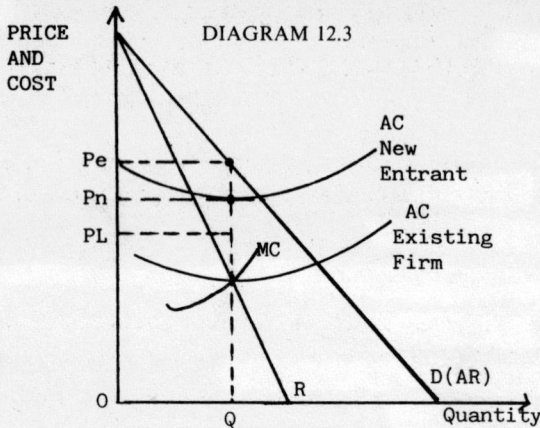

a pricing strategy which makes entry even more difficult. In diagram 12.3 the profit maximising price for existing firms is Pe, however this is above the minimum price for a new entrant enabling him to cover his Average Costs and charge price Pn. Instead the existing firm may settle for a lower monopoly profit and set price at PL, below the entry price for a new entrant.

8.3   Existing firms may have a high degree of control over the channels of distribution and may deny new entrants the means of marketing their products.

8.4   Legal barriers may exist such as patents which hamper the entry of new firms.

8.5   High levels of expenditure on research and development may act as a further barrier to the entry of new firms.

SELF ASSESSMENT QUESTIONS

1.   What is meant by oligopoly?

2.   Explain the observed price rigidity in oligopolistic markets.

3.   What is meant by non-price competition? Give examples.

4.   Explain what is meant by barriers to entry.

Chapter 13

MONOPOLISTIC COMPETITION

1.   Monopolistic competition is a form of imperfect competition and such markets are characterised by the prevalence of **BRANDED GOODS**.

2.   The market consists of:

2.1   **A PRODUCT GROUP** e.g. cigarettes, and within each product group there are:

2.2   **BRANDS** e.g. Benson & Hedges, Players, Peter Stuyvesant etc.

3.   Each producer sells a product which is slightly different from his competitors' products and will attempt to emphasise these differences; which may be real or artificial. Where no real differences exist the producer will attempt to create them by appropriate packaging and advertising. This process of creating differences is referred to as **PRODUCT DIFFERENTIATION,** and its objective is to create **BRAND LOYALTY**.

4.   The essential point to note is that each firm has a monopoly over its own brand because nobody else can produce it, however all the brands in the product group are in competition. The more the producer can convince consumers that his brand is different to his competitors, the stronger his market position will be.

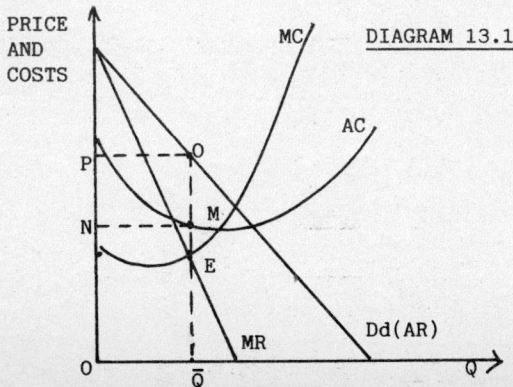

DIAGRAM 13.1

5.   In the short run monopoly profits will be made and the short run equilibrium position will be the same as under monopoly. This is illustrated in diagram 13.1 where the short-run equilibrium is at E with output $O\overline{Q}$ and price P, making monopoly profit PONM.

6.   If the barriers to entry to the industry are weak the monopoly profits will attract new entrants into the market with similar brands. This will result in a fall in the market share of each firm. In diagram 13.2 the firm's original demand curve is DD, but as new brands enter the market it is shifted to the left to D'D'.

Entry to the industry will continue until all monopoly profits have been eliminated and only normal profit is being made. In diagram 13.2 this is at point X where the demand curve D'D' is tangential to the AC curve, with costs just being covered, with price $\overline{P}$ and output q_1. Losses will occur at any other output as AC will be greater than AR, for example if output is increased to q_2 a loss indicated by the shaded area will occur, the same will be the case if output is reduced. There is therefore a long run tendency for monopoly profits to be eliminated.

7.   A further important characteristic which should be noted from diagram 13.2 is that the firm is not operating at the lowest point of its AC curve, it has the capacity to produce more, but cannot do so; and

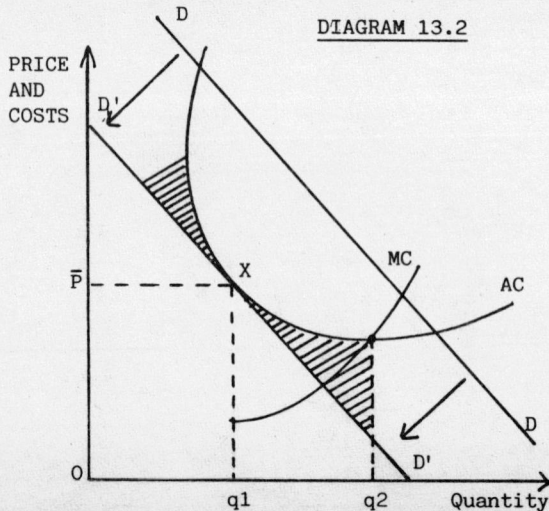

DIAGRAM 13.2

$q_1 - q_2$ represents the spare capacity of the firm. As each firm is in the same situation, one of the most important long run characteristics of monopolistically competitive industries is **EXCESS CAPACITY.**

8.   The characteristics of monopolistic competition are therefore:

8.1   A wide variety of brands.

8.2   A high level of advertising and other forms of non-price competition.

8.3   A long run tendency, in the absence of strong barriers to entry, for profits to be pushed down to zero.

8.4   Excess capacity in the industry.

SELF ASSESSMENT QUESTIONS

1.   What is a Product Group?

2.   Explain what is meant by Product Differentiation.

3.   Explain how monopoly profits are eliminated under conditions of monopolistic competition.

4.   Why do monopolistically competitive industries suffer from excess capacity?

Chapter 14
COMPETITION POLICY

1.   Control over monopoly and restrictive practices is considered to be necessary in order to promote economic efficiency and to protect the consumer against exploitation. The economic arguments against monopoly are stated in Chapter 11, we will consider here U.K. legislative measures to promote competition and prevent the worst excesses of monopoly.

2.   U.K. legislation relating to competition is directed towards:

2.1   Dominant firm monopoly.

2.2   Mergers which may create a monopoly position.

2.3   Restrictive Practices and Resale Price Maintenance.

3.   If there was a definite relationship between market structure conduct, and performance, as implied by economic theory then the solution would be to enact legislation to ban monopolies; or mergers which may result in a monopoly position. In reality however the evidence against monopolies is less clear, and in some areas gains in efficiency may outweigh the allocative costs (see Chapter 11). This has been reflected in the attitude contained within U.K. legislation towards monopoly and merger which is non-committal. There is no automatic assumption in law that monopoly is illegal per se (in itself), but rather is liable to case by case investigation, recognising that in some cases there may be benefits but at the same time attempting to control the abuses.

4.   Relevant legislation, in chronological order, is as follows:

4.1   1948 Monopolies and Restrictive Practices Act.

4.2   1956 Restrictive Practices Act (Amended 1976/77)

4.3   1964 Resale Price Maintenance Act

4.4   1965 Monopolies and Mergers Act

4.5   1980 Competition Act

5.   The main details of the relevant legislation can be summarised as follows:

5.1 Monopolies and Restrictive Practices Act 1948. Established the Monopolies Commission to investigate cases of monopoly referred to it. Its major role was to investigate and find facts relating to cases referred to it by the Department of Trade and Industry (then Board of Trade). It was essentially powerless and could only report and not take controlling action. Monopoly was defined as control of $\frac{1}{3}$ of the market share.

5.2 Restrictive Trade Practices Act 1956. This act established the **Restrictive Practices Court** and a **Registrar of Restrictive Practices** to investigate agreements between firms. Such agreements covered prices and conditions of sale or supply. Restrictive practice agreements had to be registered with the Registrar and were considered to be illegal except where they could be justified through one or more of eight "gateways" which indicated that they may be beneficial to the "public interest". Examples of these "gateways" included: the agreement was protecting the public against injury, was mainting employment or exports, made available other benefits, or counteracted restrictive measures taken by another person. By 1979 3810 restrictive agreements had been registered and only 39 had been contested, the vast majority being voluntary disbanded.

5.3 Resale Prices Act 1964. The practice of enforcing a retail price by a manufacturer on to a retailer was deemed to be illegal. The 1964 Act abolished the practice either collectively or individually, since the 1956 Act had still allowed the practice to continue on an individual basis. The Act allowed resale price maintenance to continue where the Restrictive Practices Court could be convinced that it would be in the "public interest" and that abolition would cause the public to suffer in one or more of five ways, for example: there would be a substantial reduction in the number of retail outlets, there would be a reduction in the quality or variety of goods available for sale or that there would be a danger to health as a consequence. Only certain drugs, books, and maps have been exempt.

5.4 Monopolies and Mergers Act 1965. The Act laid down that any proposed merger could be referred to the Monopolies Commission if it would result in $\frac{1}{3}$ of the market being controlled by a single firm or where the assets acquired exceeded £5 million (later raised to £15m).

5.5 **Fair Trading Act 1973.** Created the post of Director General of Fair Trading (D.G.F.T.) under whom competition and consumer law was codified and centralised. Legislation was extended to cover services such as insurance and estate agents, and the D.G.F.T. could enforce the prohibition of any practice adversely affecting consumers.

5.6 **Monopolies and Mergers Act 1973.** Amended the 1965 Act. The D.G.F.T. assumed responsibility for the operation of monopoly policy, and was empowered to refer monopolies to the re-named Monopolies and Mergers Commission. The Commission determined whether the case in question is, or is likely to be, detrimental to the public interest and to make recommendations as appropriate. Responsibility for the implementation of corrective action lies with the appropriate minister and may be by voluntary undertaking or by a binding statutory order. Monopoly was redefined as control of 25% of the market.

5.7 **Competition Act 1980.** The overall objective of the 1980 Act was to stimulate competition by controlling anti-competitive practices, and the legislation was extended to include the Nationalised Industries. The Director General was empowered to refer price issues and other specific activities to the Monopolies and Mergers Commission for investigation. Where the Commission find a practice is "against the public interest", the Secretary of State may act to control it. Investigation took place during 1980-81 into the Severn-Trent Water Authority, British Rail's commuter services and the Central Electricity Generating Board. In 1981 the role of the Commission was expanded to include the efficiency of the Nationalised Industries.

6. Monopoly legislation does not appear to have prevented the strong tendency towards market concentration in the U.K. Market concentration can be expressed by means of a **MARKET CONCENTRATION RATIO**. A five firm concentration ratio (CR^5) refers to the market share of the largest five firms, a two firm (CR^2) to the largest two firms, and so on, and is calculated as:

Market Concentration Ratio (CR^5) =
$$\frac{\text{Sales of the largest 5 firms}}{\text{Total Market Sales}}$$

The average CR^5 rose from 55.4% in 1958 to 63.4% in 1968, and 65.1% in 1975, according to product group. The data also suggests a much higher level of concentration in the U.K. than in many comparable countries within Europe, and the U.S.A.

7. The Monopolies Commission had reported on 40 monopoly situations by 1980 on a diverse range of products which included detergents, brickmaking, brewing, breakfast cereals and solicitors services. Criticism has been raised however regarding the lack of firm remedial action by the government following publication of the Commission's reports.

8. Many of the reports of the Commission have criticised the restrictive practices followed by firms. For example it was critical of the price discrimination practiced by Bird's Eye Foods when they granted retailers discounts for reserving space in freezers for their products. It was also critical of the practice of Roche products in charging excessively high prices to the National Health Service for the drugs Librium and Valium whilst other customers were paying much lower prices.

9. Policy directed towards restrictive agreement appear to have had some degree of success. Of the 4,468 agreements which had been registered by the end of 1980, 3,295 had been disbanded and of these only 39 were as a result of a judgement by the Restrictive Practices Court, the vast majority being voluntarily disbanded. This is because a judgement applies to the whole product group and once the defence for a restrictive practice is over-ruled there is little point in anyone else proceeding. It is probable therefore that many more restrictive practices would be currently in existence in the absence of the measures taken.

10. The control of mergers is intended to prevent monopoly situations from developing. During the 1970's there was a steady increase in the number of mergers falling within the criteria laid down by the Fair Trading Act as eligible for investigation. Since the 1965 legislation more than 1500 mergers have been screened however of these only 53 were referred to the Monopolies and Mergers Commission, which could be taken as evidence that the official policy is not unfavourable towards mergers. Of the mergers investigated only 18 were prohibited as being against the public

interest, and 18 were allowed to proceed provided certain assurances were given, the other 17 being abandoned.

11. The Office of Fair Trading can only investigate those arrangements where firm evidence exists and in such cases can be said to have had a fairly high degree of success. However, many formal arrangements have probably been replaced by informal arrangements or "gentlemen's agreements", for example trade associations circulating price lists and tacit agreements not to compete on price. Cases actually dealt with by the Restrictive Practices Court may not accurately reflect the actual extent to which such practices exist.

12. The apparent ineffectiveness of monopolies and mergers legislation in the U.K. may reflect the flexible, or pragmatic, nature of the underlying philosophy. In particular the criteria for the investigation of mergers is quite restrictive (£15 million assets or 25% market share) and may not cover many mergers which do have adverse effects on competition and performance. In order to make the legislation more effective it has been suggested that an assumption should be made that certain categories of merger should be assumed to be illegal with the onus on the proposers of the merger to prove that the effects would be beneficial, others would be categorised as beneficial and allowed to proceed. A further suggestion has been that a system of fines, as is the practice in the U.S.A. should be introduced for abuses of monopoly power and that the legal system should contain a stronger presumption against monopoly.

13. Competition policy in the U.K. can therefore be considered as relatively mild, reflecting a flexible attitude towards monopoly with no automatic assumption against any particular monopoly or merger, each case being treated on its merits. Legislation has therefore probably done little other than to remove the worst and most visible restrictive practices and abuses of monopoly power.

SELF ASSESSMENT QUESTIONS

1. Why is it considered necessary to have legislation for the control of monopolies and mergers?

2. Explain what is meant by the term 'restrictive practices'.

3. What is the attitude towards monopolies and mergers which is reflected in U.K. legislation?

4. What is meant by a 5 Firm Concentration Ratio?

5. How effective do you consider competition policy in the U.K. to have been?

Chapter 15
WAGES

1.   Wages are the payments received in return for labour services and as such are the returns received by **LABOUR** as a factor of production.

2.   It is necessary however to explain why it is that the **WAGE RATES** differ between occupations. In order to explain these wage differentials it is necessary to consider both demand and supply in the labour market.

3.   One explanation is the **MARGINAL PRODUCTIVITY THEORY OF WAGES**. The Law of Declining Marginal Productivity was explained in Chapter 2. It will be recalled that the Marginal Product (MP) is the addition to total output or product which occurs when one additional unit of a variable factor is added to a fixed factor. It will be recalled that MP initially rises but then starts to decline as diminishing returns set in. Total Product rises but at a declining rate. In this particular case the variable factor is labour and all other factors are fixed. The theory also makes a number of other assumptions:

   3.1   Conditions of perfect competition, therefore the firm can obtain all the labour it requires at the prevailing wage rate.

   3.2   Labour is an homogeneous factor i.e. the productivity of each unit of labour is the same.

   3.3   Perfect mobility of labour between occupations.

   3.4   The entrepreneur's aim is to maximise his profits, therefore his main concern will be the difference between the cost of employing labour and the revenue to be gained from the sale of the output of labour.

4.   **MARGINAL REVENUE PRODUCT (MRP)** refers to the addition to total revenue received from the sale of the additional unit of output, and is calculated as the marginal physical product (i.e. tonnes of potatoes etc.) multiplied by price i.e. MPP $\times$ P = MRP. As under conditions of perfect competition price is constant the MPP curve will be identical in shape to the MRP curve. (Under conditions

of imperfect competition the MRP curve is obtained by multiplying the MPP by Marginal Revenue i.e. MPP $\times$ MR = MRP).

5.   In diagram 5.1 the MRP curve can be seen to rise and then fall cutting the Average Revenue Product (ARP) curve at its highest point. The ARP curve represents the average return, in monetary terms, per unit of labour employed. As a result of the competitive

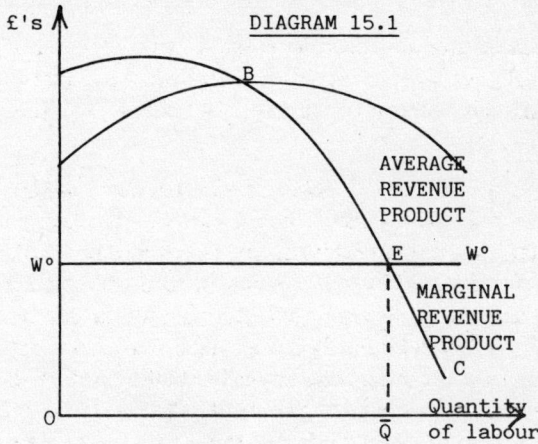

DIAGRAM 15.1

assumption the supply of labour will be perfectly elastic at the prevailing wage rate (W°) which is determined by the **MARKET** Recalling assumption 3.4 it is evident that the entrepreneur will want to employ labour as long as the MRP is greater than the wage rate (cost of labour), in diagram 15.1 he will continue to employ additional labour up to O$\overline{\text{Q}}$ as this will add more to revenue than to costs. Above O$\overline{\text{Q}}$ additional labour will cost more than its MRP and will not therefore be employed. The profit maximising entrepreneur will therefore employ O$\overline{\text{Q}}$ labour. If we consider the wage rate to be the marginal cost of labour we can see that the conclusion is another form of the MR = MC rule encountered under the theory of the firm, point E being the equilibrium point.

6.   The relevant section of the MRP curve is however B — C only. This is because no firm would employ labour when the wage rate is greater than the ARP as the profit maximising entrepreneur would never pay more to **ALL** workers than the highest ARP, as losses would result. The section of the MRP curve below·ARP i.e.

B — C can be considered as the competitive firm's **DEMAND CURVE FOR LABOUR.**

7. MRP theory is therefore a theory of how the **DEMAND** for labour is determined, but as the supply of labour is excluded it cannot be considered as a theory of how wages are determined as it says nothing about the determination of wage rates.

8. MRP theory however can be useful as a tool for analysing the effects on the demand for labour of the changes in the relevant variables. In diagram 15.2 an increase in the wage rate from W° to W'

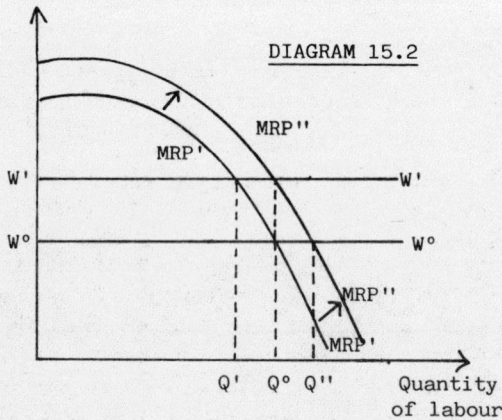

DIAGRAM 15.2

will result in a reduction in the quantity of labour employed from Q° to Q'. If however the MRP curve can be shifted upwards and outwards from MRP' to MRP" then the quantity of labour can remain unchanged at Q°. Alternatively if the shift in the MRP curve takes place with the wage rate remaining constant at W° the amount of labour employed would increase to Q" or the existing work force Q° could enjoy the higher wage rate. Shifts in the MRP curve from MRP' to MRP" can be brought about by:

8.1 An increase in productivity brought about by the abandonment of a previously held restrictive practice.

8.2 The adoption of new technology which makes labour more productive.

8.3 An increase in the price of the product — which may be difficult given the competitive assumption.

9.   The demand for labour has four characteristics which affect the extent to which the labour force can affect the wage rate.

9.1   The demand for labour is a **DERIVED DEMAND**. i.e. The demand for labour is derived from the product it produces, the greater the demand fot the product the greater the demand for labour.

9.2   The elasticity of demand for labour is derived from the elasticity of demand for the product; the greater the elasticity of demand for the product the greater the elasticity of demand for the labour producing it.

9.3   The proportion of total cost accounted for by labour — the lower this is the more scope labour will have to gain increases in wages.

9.4   The extent to which capital can be substituted for labour in the production process, the easier this is the weaker will be the position of labour.

10.   The wage rate in a particular occupation is determined by the interaction of demand and supply in that particular labour market. The labour market is not a single homogeneous market but consists of thousands of different markets each with its own particular supply curve. The elasticity of the labour supply curve will depend upon factors such as the amount of training and skill required and the duration of the training period required. The supply curve may be more inelastic due to restrictions upon entry to an occupation, where for example, Trade Unions insist upon lengthy apprenticeships.

Diagram 15.3 represents the supply curve for a relatively unskilled occupation where an increase in the wage rate from W' to W"

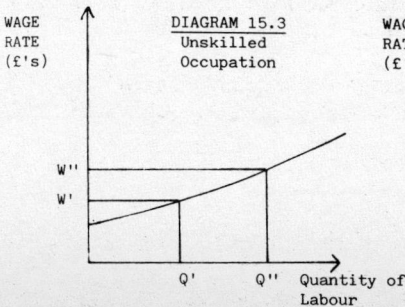

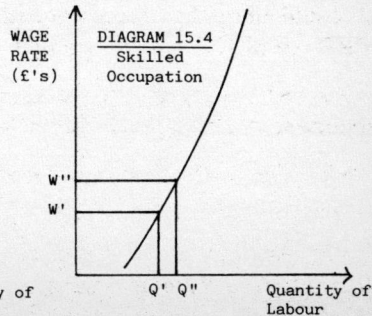

WAGE RATE (£'s)

DIAGRAM 15.3
Unskilled
Occupation

W"
W'

Q'   Q"   Quantity of Labour

WAGE RATE (£'s)

DIAGRAM 15.4
Skilled
Occupation

W"
W'

Q' Q"   Quantity of Labour

substantially increases the supply of labour from Q' to Q''. The same magnitude of increase in the skilled occupation, represented in diagram 15.4, has a far less significant effect upon the supply of labour, Q' to Q'', due to the training period required to acquire the necessary skills, or restrictions placed upon entry.

11. Other points for consideration which wage theory does not incorporate, but may affect wages, include:

11.1 Legislation such as the Sex Discrimination and Equal Pay Acts 1975.

11.2 Incomes Policies, under which Governments have attempted to control the rate of wage increase according to some predetermined "norm".

11.3 Government management of the economy and the effects of inflationary/deflationary measures, and tax policy.

12. **THE BARGAINING THEORY OF WAGES** views wages as being the outcome of negotiations between two powerful monopoly groups, on the one hand the Trade Unions who monopolise the supply of labour, and on the other the employers' organisations who monopolise the demand. The relative bargaining strengths of the two parties will vary between different time periods according to changes in the economic climate. For example during recession the employers will be in the stronger bargaining position and during economic boom when the demand for labour is high the Trade Unions will be in a stronger position.

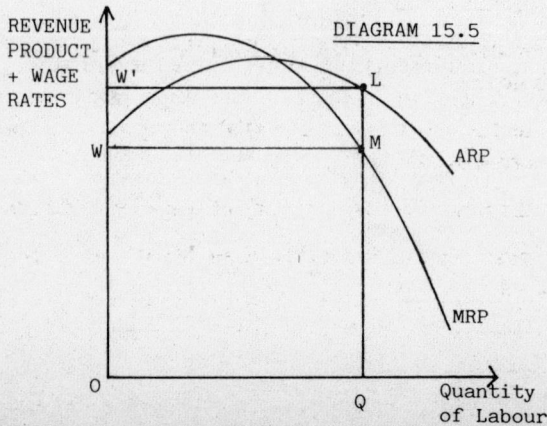

DIAGRAM 15.5

13. Bargaining theory can however be incorporated within marginal productivity theory. In diagram 15.5 the current wage rate is OW, and recalling that the entrepreneur will never pay a wage greater than the ARP of labour, we can see that the highest wage which would be paid is OW' (QL). LM is the surplus earned by the entrepreneur on each worker employed (OQ). A wage increase above OW would normally reduce the quantity of labour employed. If however the workforce is strongly unionised they may be able to resist the reduction in the workforce and persuade the employer to pay the increase out of his surplus L — M. The extent to which L — M will be shared with the workforce depends upon relative bargaining strengths at the time.

14. Despite the criticisms of marginal productivity theory the principles it contains appear to be inescapable in the long run and it does appear that any wage increases which are considerably above the rate of productivity increase will result in a reduction in the size of the work force. Marginal productivity is therefore probably always present at the bargaining table, whether the parties to the bargain are aware of it or not; but there are so many other factors influencing wages that it is probably not a fully adequate explanation of any particular wage rate.

SELF ASSESSMENT QUESTIONS

1. Which section of the MRP curve represents the firm's demand curve for labour?

2. How does the competitive firm decide how much labour to employ?

3. State the weaknesses of MRP theory as a theory of wage determination.

4. Outline an alternative theory of wage determination.

5. Discuss the factors other than MRP which may influence wages.

Chapter 16
RENT

1.   Rent in everyday terms refers to a regular payment made in return for the use of an asset, in economics however the term has a far more specific meaning. In economics rent refers to the **PAYMENT TO A FACTOR OF PRODUCTION WHICH IS IN FIXED SUPPLY.**

2.   The concept of economic rent was originally applied to land only. David Ricardo was one of the earliest economists to discuss the theory. Ricardo noted that as the supply of land was fixed, with no way of increasing or decreasing it, supply could not respond to changes in demand. If this was the case what then determined the price of the land? The **'SUPPLY PRICE'** refers to the minimum payment which is necessary to keep a factor of production in its current use, and as the supply of land cannot be varied it has no supply price. Any payment to a factor of production which is above the supply price is a surplus, and is referred to as **ECONOMIC RENT. RENT THEREFORE IS ANY SURPLUS ABOVE THE SUPPLY PRICE.** As land is perfectly inelastic in supply, and therefore has no supply price, the whole of the return to the landlord for his land is economic rent, i.e.

ECONOMIC RENT = CURRENT EARNINGS — SUPPLY PRICE

3.   During the Napoleonic Wars grain prices rose to very high levels and many people blamed this on the high price, and therefore rents, of argicultural land. Ricardo however pointed out the flaw in this explanation. As the supply of land was fixed and therefore could not vary with demand the price of land could not determine grain prices. The only demand for land is in fact a **DERIVED DEMAND**, derived from the demand for grain. If the demand for grain is high the price is high, which enables the landlord to charge a higher rent for grain growing land. Should the demand for grain fall however, the landlord would be forced to take whatever rent he could obtain as the land would still be there even if the return was zero. In reality of course land has alternative uses and at some point it may be more profitable to transfer it to some alternative use such as potatoes.

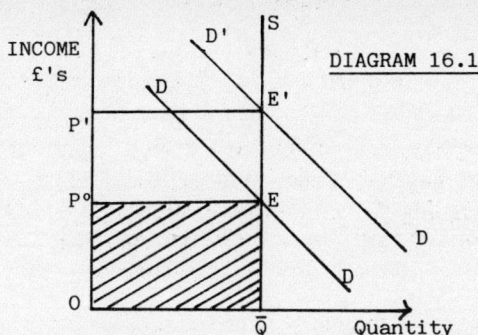

INCOME
£'s

DIAGRAM 16.1

4. Diagram 16.1 illustrates the concept of pure economic rent. The supply of the factor of production is fixed at $O\overline{Q}$ with demand DD and price P°, the shaded area $OP°E\overline{Q}$ is economic rent. An increase in the demand for the factor to D'D' increases the rent by P°P'E'E. As the supply has remained unchanged at $O\overline{Q}$ all of the additional factor income is rent.

5. Diagram 16.1 could be used to illustrate the supply of individuals with unique talents, for example certain entertainers, footballers and other sportsmen, great actors or skilful entrepreneurs. Such talents earn what it referred to as **RENT OF ABILITY**.

6. When a factor is in temporarily fixed supply, for example a class of skilled labour, and economic rents will be earned in the short-run only, in this case until more people can be trained; then the rent is referred to as **QUASI-RENT**.

7. Although the amount of land, or any other factor, may be fixed, in reality it is unlikely to be specific to a single use only and may be transferred to alternative uses. For example, argricultural land may be used as building land, or transferred to alternative agricultural uses. The minimum payment which is necessary to retain a factor of production in its current use and prevent it from transferring to its next best alternative is known as its **TRANSFER EARNINGS**. Transfer earnings can be considered as the opportunity cost of keeping a factor in its current use. Where a factor has alternative uses **ANY PAYMENT MADE OVER THE FACTOR'S TRANSFER EARNINGS IS ECONOMIC RENT**. For example a footballer earning £500 per week who has also trained as a plumber, and could earn £100 per week at plumbing. If his earnings as a footballer began

to fall he would transfer to plumbing when his wages as a footballer fell below £100.

8.   Wherever a factor of production has an upward sloping supply curve part of its earnings will be rent and part transfer earnings. The proportions of rent and transfer earnings depend upon the elasticity of supply of the factor. The less elastic is the supply the greater the proportion of economic rent, the greater the elasticity of supply the greater are the transfer earnings. In the extreme case of zero elasticity of supply all the return is rent and where elasticity of supply is infinity it is all transfer earnings.

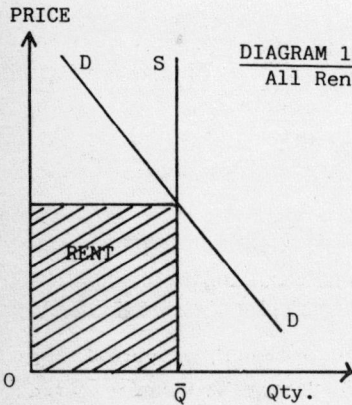

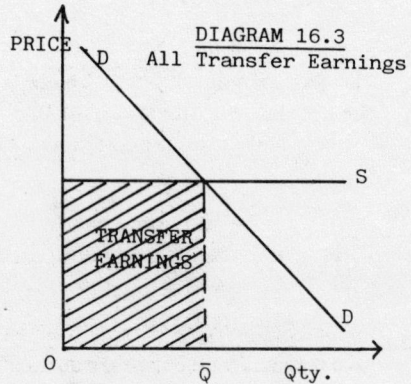

DIAGRAM 16.2 — All Rent

DIAGRAM 16.3 — All Transfer Earnings

In diagram 16.4 the factor earnings are equally divided between Rent and Transfer Earnings.

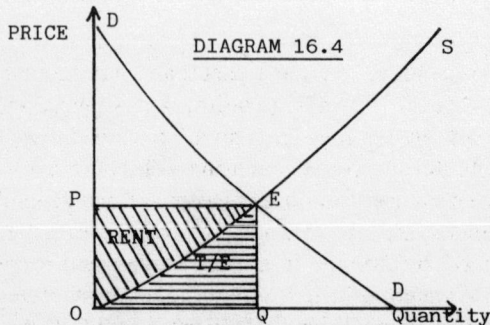

DIAGRAM 16.4

9.   City centre land sites are extremely expensive, which is a consequence of the highly inelastic supply. The supply of such sites is extremely restricted and each site has many competing uses. Demand

is continually rising but the supply of sites for cinemas, restaurants, car parks, offices and shops cannot be increased. The high price of such sites results from the increasing demand and inelastic supply, however as the sites have many alternative uses the element of rent in the price for any particular use will be quite small, the greatest element being transfer earnings. The earnings in any particular use will have to be at least sufficient to prevent it from transferring to the next best alternative, for example, the high price of cinema tickets in city centres reflects the need for cinemas to earn sufficient returns to prevent them from being transferred to use as restuarants or offices.

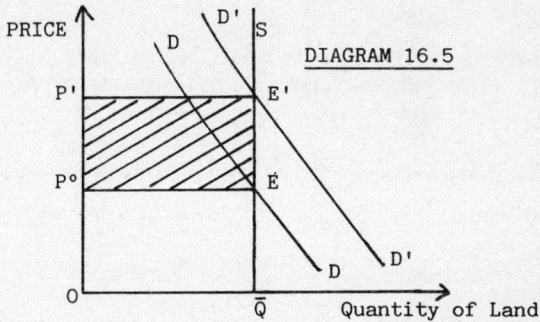

DIAGRAM 16.5

In diagram 16.5 demand curve DD represents the demand for an urban site for use as a restaurant, for which the price would be P° and D'D' the demand for the same site as a cinema, for which the market price which people are willing to pay is P'. Only the shaded area P°P'E'E, the surplus over the next best alternative use, is economic rent.

10.   It has been suggested in the past that the economic rents earned on land should be the basis for taxation. This suggestion is frequently associated with Henry George, who advocated the use of such a tax in the U.S.A. during the 19th century. The land tax was to be the single source of taxation and was justified on the grounds that as the supply of land is fixed the returns to the owner may rise without any extra effort on his behalf. It was this 'unearned increment' upon which the tax was to be levied, and as the supply of land was fixed the tax could not be avoided (i.e. the 'tax base' could not be eroded). The proposal to tax the economic rent on land has two main difficulties:

10.1   How to distinguish between rent and transfer earnings.

10.2　The problem of identifying the element of rent, recalling that the amount of commercial rent paid to the landlord is not the same as economic rent.

Similar arguments to those used in favour of the land tax have been used in support of the arguments to tax the rent element in the earnings of individuals with unique talents such as 'pop singers', entertainers and footballers.

11.　The essential points to bear in mind are:

11.1　**RENTS DO NOT DETERMINE PRICES, IT IS PRICES WHICH DETERMINE RENTS.**

11.2　**RENT IS A SURPLUS WHICH BECOMES GREATER AS THE PRICE OF THE PRODUCT FROM WHICH THE DEMAND FOR THE FACTOR IS DERIVED INCREASES.**

SELF ASSESSMENT QUESTIONS

1. Distinguish between economic rent and rent in its everyday context.

2. Outline the factors which determine economic rent.

3. Distinguish between rent and transfer earnings.

4. What is meant by Quasi-Rent?

5. Why are house prices in city centres higher than elsewhere?

Chapter 17
INTEREST

1. Interest is the factor reward, or earnings, of **CAPITAL**. Alternatively it can be considered as the payment for the use of money. This money may be used for the purchase of capital equipment, but may also be used for alternative purposes. This source of finance will only be available if other people are willing to forego consumption and provide a pool of financial resources from which loans can be made. This supply of funds will only be forthcoming if those supplying the funds receive some reward for sacrificing their current consumption and are compensated for the risks involved; in particular the possibility of not getting their money back, or the possibility of a reduction in the value of their money due to inflation. Interest can therefore be considered as the price of borrowing money.

2. The **DEMAND** for **CAPITAL** can be analysed in a manner which is almost identical to the Marginal Productivity of Labour Theory of Wages.

If the stock of capital is increased relative to other factors of production diminishing returns will eventually set in as capital, like the other factors of production, is subject to the Law of Diminishing

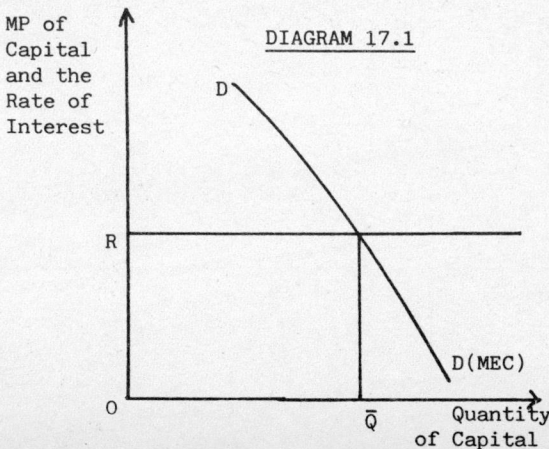

DIAGRAM 17.1

Marginal Productivity. The Marginal Productivity of Capital Curve in Diagram 17.1 represents the firm's demand for capital curve. This is known also as the **MARGINAL EFFICIENCY OF CAPITAL CURVE.** It slopes downwards due to diminishing returns and as the rate of interest is the cost of capital the capital stock will be expanded to just the point at which the cost is equal to the value of the marginal product. The firm will therefore employ $\overline{OQ}$ capital at interest rate R. Profitability is therefore maximised when: **MP OF CAPITAL = RATE OF INTEREST.**

As was the case in the analysis of wages, a change in either the physical productivity of capital or in the price of goods produced will bring about a shift in the MP curve and therefore the demand for capital.

Analysis is in fact more complicated than this as investment decisions are taken on the basis of anticipated returns from the investment over the lifetime of the capital compared with the current outlay. This approach requires the use of discounting to obtain the 'present value' of the investment's yield. (For further details see any slightly more advanced text or the companion volume to this text.)

3. If the rate of interest is the 'price' of borrowed funds then if we wish to formulate a theory of how interest rates are determined we must also consider the supply of funds for lending. The theory that the interest rate is determined by the demand and supply for loanable funds is referred to as the **CLASSICAL THEORY** of interest rate determination.

4. The supply of loanable funds for investment is determined by current savings. The supply curve in Diagram 17.2 is society's savings function the shape of which represents the **TIME PREFERENCE** of individuals i.e. the extent to which present consumption is preferred

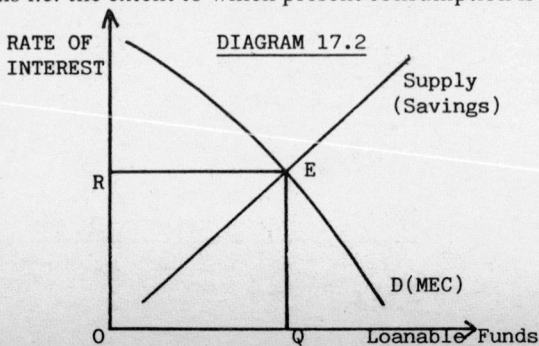

DIAGRAM 17.2

to future consumption. A rate of interest is necessary to compensate savers for the loss of current purchasing power. A rate of interest is therefore necessary in order to induce savings. The intersection of the demand and supply curves gives the equilibrium rate of interest. If desired saving is greater than the demand for investment purposes there will be an excess supply of savings which will push down the rate of interest until equilibrium between demand and supply is re-established. If demand exceeds supply the rate of interest will rise until sufficient extra savings are forthcoming to re-establish an equilibrium.

5.   Classical Theory is referred to as a 'flow theory' because it assumes that a continuous flow of savings is possible at the prevailing rate of interest.

5.1   According to Classical Theory savings are not assumed to be a function of (dependent upon) the level of income.

(There are several other theories of interest rate determination which are discussed in the companion text to this book entitled Basic Concepts in Macro Economics.)

6.   The major determinants of saving are as follows:

6.1   The level of income. As incomes rise the proportion of income devoted to consumption tends to decline, hence in economies where incomes are high the proportion of saving tends to be higher.

6.2   The extent to which the financial structure of the economy has developed thereby providing a range of institutions where savings can be safely deposited and where they can earn an adequate return with a minimum of risk.

6.3   The extent to which a society views thrift as being a virtue or otherwise. This can vary between different societies, or within the same society over different time periods. In Victorian times thrift was seen as being far more virtuous than it is in the present day.

7.   Savings can be of several different types.

7.1   Personal Savings consist of the money which households choose not to spend from their personal disposable incomes, which may be with the intention of acquiring some specific item, for example a car, or merely out of habit.

7.2   Corporate Savings consist largely of the retained profits of firms.

7.3   Private Savings consist of 7.1 and 7.2 together.

7.4   Government Savings occur when the Government gathers more in tax revenue than it spends, and is in a sense 'forced saving'.

7.5   A large proportion of saving is contractual in that it consists of payments to insurance companies for life assurance or payments into pension funds.

It is unlikely that the rate of interest has any more than a marginal effect on any of these saving motives.

8.   Experience of the 1960's and 1970's suggest that the growth of income is a significant influence upon savings behaviour. In 1969 the Savings Ratio (the ratio of personal savings to personal disposable income) was 8.1, this rose to 15.4 in 1980, before declining again as the rate of growth of incomes declined.

SELF ASSESSMENT QUESTIONS

1.   How is the demand curve for capital derived?

2.   What is meant by the 'time preference' of individuals and what is its relationship to the supply of loanable funds?

3.   Describe the function of the rate of interest.

4.   Outline the 'Classical Theory' of interest rate determination.

Chapter 18
PROFITS

1.   Profit is the reward to the entrepreneur. This factor payment is the return to the entrepreneur for

1.1   Co-ordinating and setting to work the factors of production.

1.2   Taking the risk of losing his capital.

2.   **RISK** is always present in capitalist production as production has to take place in advance of sale and it can never be known with certainty that the goods will actually be sold. Profit is therefore the reward for uncertainty bearing and differs from interest in the degree of risk involved; interest is associated with investments which are virtually risk free.

3.   At this stage it is useful to recall the different concepts of profit:

3.1   Normal Profit (Chapter 10)

3.2   Super Normal Profit (Chapter 10)

3.3   Monopoly Profit (Chapter 11)

4.   The difference between profits and the other forms of factor income is that it is a **RESIDUAL** which is paid after the other factors of production have been paid out, and may therefore be **NEGATIVE**. Also because factor costs and sales cannot be controlled or forecast profit tends to **FLUCTUATE** more than the other factor incomes.

5.   The functions of profit in a free market economy are as follows:

5.1   To ensure a supply of individuals willing to accept the risks of uncertainty.

5.2   Super Normal Profits indicate to entrepreneurs which industries should expand and which should contract. Therefore Super Normal Profits reflect consumers' preferences for a good, and encourages the increased output of these goods which are in demand by consumers.

5.3   Profits provide the resources necessary for expansion, both by re-investment in the firm. and by enabling the firm to offer higher rewards to the factors of production and attract them away from declining industries.

5.4   Profits overcome the technical problems of how goods are to be produced by ensuring that production is carried on by only the most efficient firms. In a competitive industry the firms making the largest profits are those with the lowest costs, if other firms are to survive they will be forced to adopt the same methods of production, otherwise their prices will be too high and they will not be able to compete. Eventually they will make losses and go out of business, or leave the industry.

SELF ASSESSMENT QUESTIONS

1.   Distinguish between Normal Profit, Super Normal Profit and Monopoly Profit.

2.   In what sense is profit a residual?

3.   What does the entrepreneur do in return for profit?

4.   How does profit differ from interest?

5.   What are the functions of profit?

6.   What is meant by the statement "Profit is a residual of uncertain size"?

Chapter 19
CONSUMER BEHAVIOUR

1. Consumers will allocate their incomes between their chosen 'basket of goods' in a manner which maximises the utility (satisfaction) they receive from their expenditures.

2. Consumers compare the utilities they receive from various quantities of the goods they are considering buying to their prices. They will achieve the maximum satisfaction when the ratio of marginal utility to price between each good is equal. i.e.

$$\frac{\text{MARGINAL UTILITY GOOD 1}}{\text{PRICE OF GOOD 1}} = \frac{\text{MARGINAL UTILITY GOOD 2}}{\text{PRICE OF GOOD 2}} = \frac{\text{MARGINAL UTILITY GOOD 3}}{\text{PRICE OF GOOD 3}} \ldots\ldots \frac{\text{MARGINAL UTILITY GOOD N}}{\text{PRICE OF GOOD N}}$$

which can be alternately represented as:

$$\frac{\text{MU GOOD 1}}{P_1} = \frac{\text{MU GOOD 2}}{P_2} = \frac{\text{MU GOOD 3}}{P_3} \ldots\ldots\ldots \frac{\text{MU}_n}{P_n}$$

3. It can be intuitively reasoned that if a consumer could gain more utility by transferring expenditure from one good to another he would do so until the point where no further utility could be gained by re-arranging expenditures. At this point the MU to Price ratios have been equalised.

4. In order to analyse the conditions for the consumer to be in equilibrium when faced with a given income and different relative prices we can utilise **INDIFFERENCE CURVE** analysis.

5. Indifference Curves represent different combinations of goods available to a consumer, each combination yielding equal

TABLE 19.1

	GOOD A	GOOD B
1	35	5
2	20	10
3	10	15
4	5	35

satisfaction to the consumer. As each combination of goods yields equal satisfaction the consumer is said to be indifferent regarding which actual combination he chooses. Table 19.1 represents different combinations of two goods A and B which will yield equal utility to the consumer. There would of course by many other possible combinations but here we have shown only four out of all those possible. As each of the combinations yield equal satisfaction the consumer will be indifferent as to which he actually chooses. These combinations are represented graphically in Diagram 19.1. In Diagram 19.1 the indifference curve II represents the four combinations of A and B shown in Table 19.1. Each point on the curve would be equally desirable to the consumer and he would be indifferent to any combination available to him along the curve. The shape of the curve is concave when viewed from the origin reflecting the "Law of Substitution". As one of the goods becomes scarcer as we move along the curve the greater becomes its relative substitution value, and its marginal utility rises relative to that of the good which has become more plentiful; and the good which is becoming relatively scarcer requires larger quantities of the other good in return. The lines L - M represent the exchange terms at that point on the curve i.e. 3:1. This is the **MARGINAL RATE OF SUBSTITUTION** of A for B, which will maintain a constant level of utility along the curve.

6.   The indifference curve in diagram 19.1 is however drawn for a single level of income only and as the consumer moves to higher

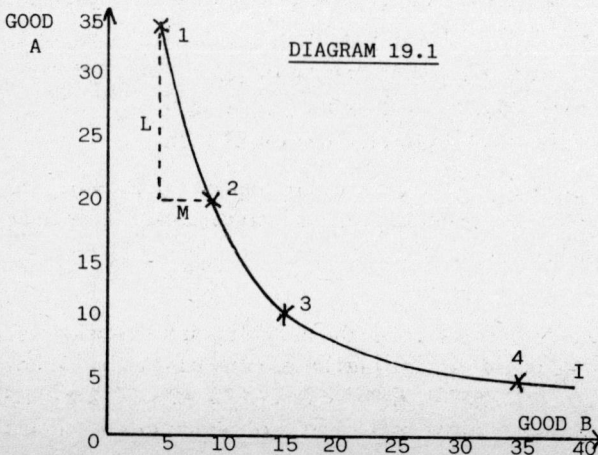

DIAGRAM 19.1

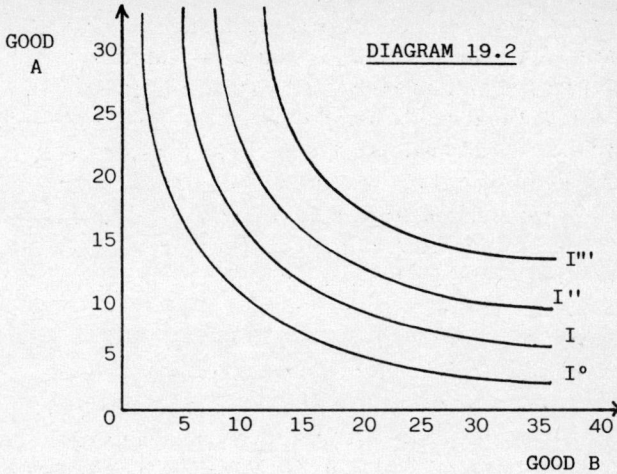

GOOD A

DIAGRAM 19.2

GOOD B

levels of income he will move to higher levels of satisfaction, and therefore a higher indifference curve. Diagram 19.2 represents the **INDIFFERENCE MAP,** each indifference curve being relevant to a different level of income. The consumer will be indifferent between different combinations along any single curve, but as income increases he can move to a higher curve. There is an infinite number on each curve, one for each possible level of income.

7.   The indifference map refers only to **CONSUMERS PREFERENCES** if we are to establish which bundle of goods will actually be preferred we need also to consider the relative prices of the two goods, and the consumer's income. If we assume that:

(i)   **CONSUMER'S INCOME IS £40,**
(ii)   **THE PRICE OF GOOD A is £1 each,**
(iii)   **THE PRICE OF GOOD B is £2 each,**

we can estimate the various quantities of each good which are available to the consumer given his income constraint and the prices of the two goods.

Table 19.2 illustrates some of the possible combinations of A and B. Clearly if 40 of Good A are purchased there will be no income left for expenditure on Good B, and vice versa if 20 units of B are purchased. Between these two extremes various combinations are available.

TABLE 19.2

GOOD A	GOOD B
40	0
30	5
20	10
10	15
0	20

8. From the data in section 7 we can derive the consumer's **BUDGET LINE**. This is illustrated in Diagram 19.3 by the line D-F

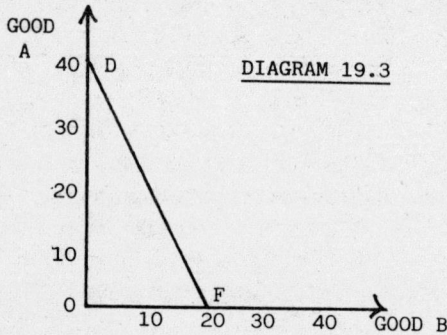

DIAGRAM 19.3

and represents all the possible combinations of the two goods which can be purchased assuming the entire income is spent on the two

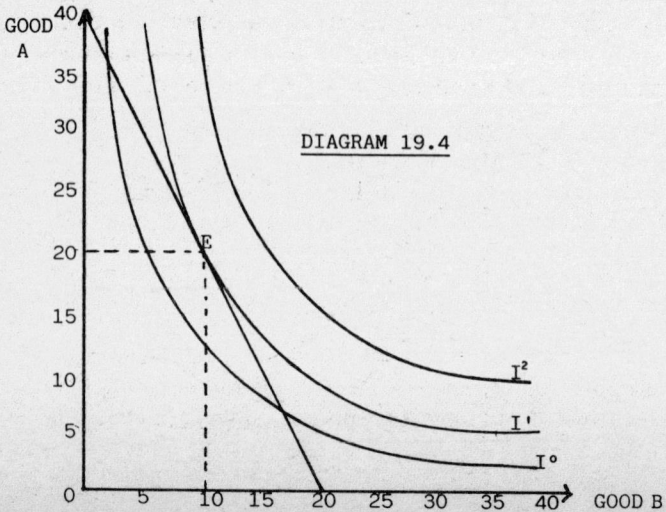

DIAGRAM 19.4

goods. The slope of line D-F being the ratio of the price of Good A to Good B. It is important to note at this stage that the Budget Line represents what is **AVAILABLE TO THE CONSUMER NOT HIS PREFERENCES.**

9.   In order to establish which combination will be preferred, or **CONSUMER EQUILIBRIUM,** it is necessary to combine the consumer's indifference map with his Budget Line. The £40 budget line from diagram 19.3 is combined with the indifference map from diagram 19.2. The point of **CONSUMER'S EQUILIBRIUM** is at E in diagram 19.4 with 20 units of Good A and 10 units of Good B. The consumer is in equilibrium where the highest attainable indifference curve is just tangential to the budget constraint. The consumer cannot move to a higher indifference curve on his current income, and he will not move to a lower one as he will not be maximising his utility. At point E the consumer's Marginal Rate of Substitution (MRS) of A for B is exactly equal to the ratio of the price of A to the price of B, from which it is evident that the condition for consumer equilibrium is

$$MRS_{AB} = \frac{P_A}{P_B}$$

10.   A reduction in income, or an equal rise in the price of both goods — which amounts to the same thing — will result in a shift of the budget line inwards towards the origin; the shift is parallel because the relative prices of the two goods are unchanged. In diagram 19.5 this is shown by the shift of the budget line D-F to NM.

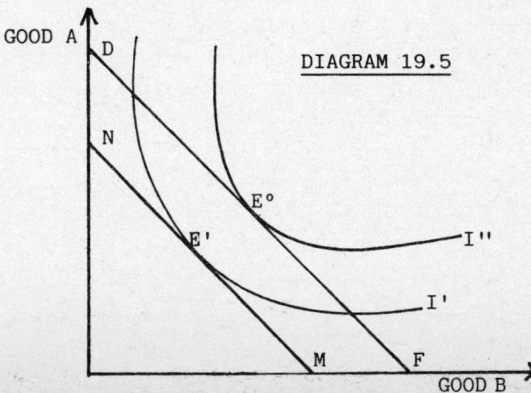

DIAGRAM 19.5

Assuming both goods are normal goods there will be a new equilibrium at E' where the new budget line is tangential to the highest attainable indifference curve I', with fewer of both goods purchased.

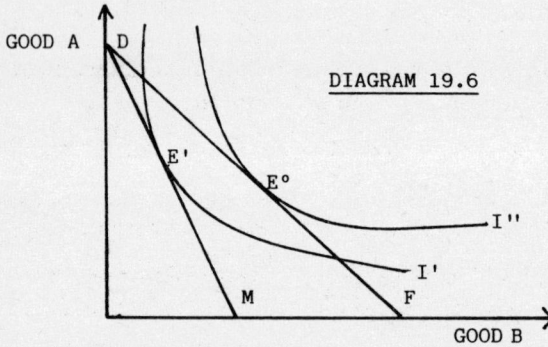

GOOD A D

DIAGRAM 19.6

E'

E°

I''

I'

M   F

GOOD B

11.   An increase in the price of one good will shift the budget line in towards the origin. In diagram 19.6 the price of good B rises and the budget line shifts from DF to DM, the slope of the line changes because the relative prices of the two goods have changed. This leaves the consumer on the lower indifference curve I' with a new equilibrium at E'. As one good becomes cheaper relative to another, and provided both are normal goods, then more of the good which has become cheaper will be purchased in place of that which has become relatively more expensive. This is referred to as the **SUBSTITUTION EFFECT,** and in the diagram it can be seen that at E' more of **GOOD** A is purchased than previously. Any price change also has an effect on **REAL INCOME,** in this example the price increases reduces real income and means that fewer of **ALL** goods can be purchased (and vice versa for a price reduction), this is referred to as the **INCOME EFFECT** of a price change. The **SUBSTITUTION EFFECT** is represented by a movement **ALONG** the indifference curve whilst the **INCOME EFFECT** is represented by a **SHIFT TO ANOTHER INDIFFERENCE CURVE.** All price changes consist of **BOTH** an income effect and a substitution effect and for all normal goods the income effect reinforces the substitution effect. However, for those inferior goods referred to as **GIFFIN GOODS** (see Chapter 4) a negative income effect may outweigh the substitution effect, in which case an increase in price may result in

MORE of the good being purchased, and for a price reduction **LESS** being purchased. This provides a theoretical explanation for the regression in the demand curve for such goods, outlined in Chapter 4.

SELF ASSESSMENT QUESTIONS

1. What condition is necessary for a consumer to receive the maximum utility from his expenditure?

2. Outline the method of construction and the significance of indifference curves.

3. What is meant by the consumer's budget line?

4. Using indifference curve analysis illustrate the conditions necessary for a consumer to be in equilibrium.

5. Illustrate how consumers' equilibrium is affected by:
   i) A fall in the price of one good
   ii) An increase in income.

Chapter 20
ALTERNATIVE THEORIES OF THE FIRM

1.   The theories of the firm discussed so far are all based on the assumption that firms will always be motivated purely by the desire to maximise their short-run profits. In many firms today however, there is a clear division between the ownership and control of the organisation. Ownership is spread amongst shareholders whilst control over day to day decision making is in the hands of paid managers, and although some of the senior management, such as directors, may also have a minority shareholding, the majority of shares are held by individuals who have little or no contact with the firm on a regular basis and may only wish to exert influence through their votes at the Annual General Meeting of shareholders — if they are sufficiently interested to bother attending.

2.   The division between ownership and control of the organisation allows for the possibility that **MANAGERS MAY PURSUE SOME ALTERNATIVE OBJECTIVE THAN PROFIT MAXIMISATION.** The alternative theories of the firm fall into two categories:

2.1 Those which assume that managers attempt to **MAXIMISE SOME OBJECTIVE OTHER THAN PROFITS,** referred to as **MANAGERIAL THEORIES** of the firm.

2.2. Those which allow for the possibility that **MANAGERS DO NOT ATTEMPT TO MAXIMISE ANY VARIABLE** but are motivated by some **ALTERNATIVE OBJECTIVE,** referred to as **BEHAVIOURAL THEORIES** of the firm.

3.   **BAUMOL**[1] proposed a model of the firm based upon the principle that the primary objective of the managers of a firm is to **MAXIMISE SALES REVENUE.** Managers may seek to maximise sales revenue for a variety of reasons but mainly because the status and salaries of managers are generally linked to the growth of sales, as their **PERFORMANCE IS FREQUENTLY JUDGED BY THE GROWTH OF SALES RATHER THAN PROFITABILITY.** In this model the need to make profits is still recognised but they act as a **CONSTRAINT ON MANAGERIAL BEHAVIOUR** rather than as an objective. It is recognised that there is a minimum level of profit which is necessary to meet the expectations of shareholders hence

sales can be maximised subject to the constraint of earning this minimum level of profit. Sales maximisation does not refer to the maximisation of sales volume but the maximisation of sales revenue.

4.   The Sales Maximisation model is illustrated in Diagram 20.1. In the diagram profit is maximised at output Q^1 where the difference between Total Cost and Total Revenue is greatest, coinciding with the profit maximising rule of MC = MR (see Chapter 10, Appendix 2). The line Pc represents the firm's profit constraint which is the minimum level of profit necessary to satisfy shareholders. The sales maximising firm will therefore increase output beyond Q^1

DIAGRAM 20.1

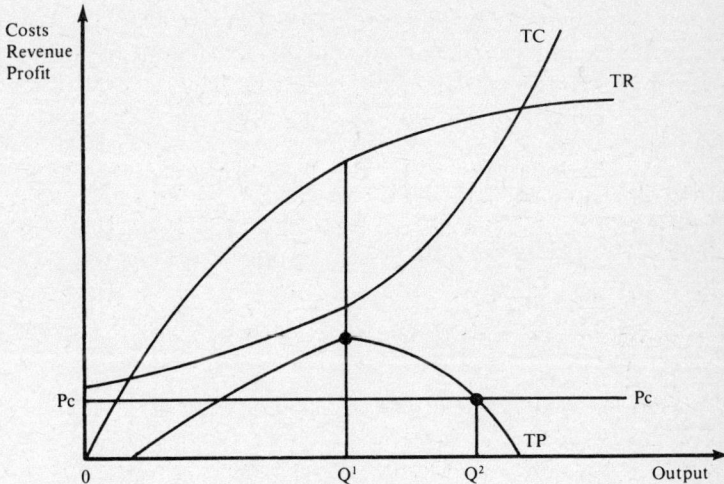

up to the point where rising costs reduce profits to the level of the profit constraint which is output Q^2 in the diagram. The model therefore predicts that the **OUTPUT OF THE SALES MAXIMISING FIRM WILL BE GREATER THAN THAT ASSUMED UNDER THE PROFIT MAXIMISING RULE.** The only way in which the two outputs could coincide would be if the profit constraint was set at the point of profit maximisation.

5.   The Baumol model also suggests a **RELATIONSHIP BETWEEN THE FIRM'S ADVERTISING BUDGET AND ITS CHOICE OF OBJECTIVES.** This relationship is illustrated in Diagram 20.2. In the diagram the shape of the total revenue curve

assumes that the physical volume of sales can always be increased by advertising but eventually diminishing returns set in and it is assumed that total revenue will vary in exactly the same way so any increase in physical sales volume resulting from increased advertising expenditure must always be accompanied by a proportionate increase in total revenue. The firm's other costs are assumed to be a function of advertising outlay and are added to advertising costs to obtain the total cost curve CC. The total profits curve TP is derived by subtracting total cost from sales revenue at each level of advertising expenditure. The line Pc is the profit constraint as described earlier.

DIAGRAM 20.2

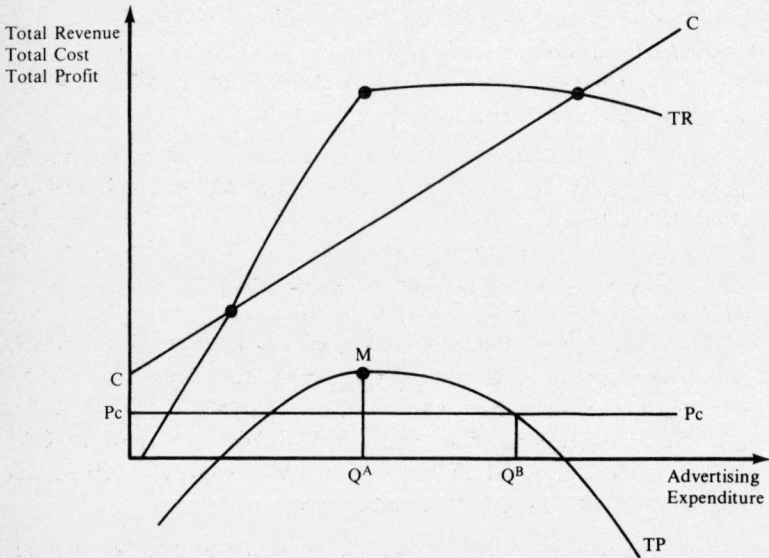

The advertising budget for the profit maximising firm is Q^A where total profit is maximised at M; however the constrained sales maximising firm will increase the advertising budget to the point where total profit just meets the profit constraint (Pc) i.e. advertising budget Q^B. The constrained sales revenue maximising firm will therefore advertise more than the profit maximising firm, because advertising will increase the sales volume and hence sales revenue, and advertising expenditure will increase to the point where the firm comes into conflict with the profit constraint.

6. **O. WILLIAMSON**[2] developed a **MANAGERIAL UTILITY MODEL OF THE FIRM** based upon **MANAGERIAL DISCRETION** within large corporations. The model is based upon the assumption that shareholders do not exert direct control over the management of the firm and that the firm is not operating in a highly competitive market. Given these assumptions **MANAGERS PURSUE THEIR OWN GOALS, SUBJECT TO THEIR BEING ABLE TO MAINTAIN CONTROL OF THE FIRM.** The goals of the firm therefore reflect the goals of the individual managers. The goals of the firm's managers are expressed in a managerial utility function which consists of three broad groups of expenditure:

6.1 **MANAGERIAL SALARIES.**

6.2 **DISCRETIONARY INVESTMENT SPENDING** on, for example, lavish offices and furniture.

6.3 **EXPENDITURES ON THE NUMBER OF STAFF** reporting to a particular manager.

The greater the profits of the firm the more managers have the ability to undertake these forms of expenditure; hence **PROFITS ARE IMPORTANT IN THE MODEL.** However, the ability to undertake such expenditure also depends upon the ability of management to divert profits from shareholders. This is not a problem, however, as shareholders do not involve themselves in the management of the firm, and consist of a fragmented group which can be kept largely in ignorance of the detailed finances of the firm by the senior managements; which implies that **MANAGERS WILL ENJOY A CONSIDERABLE DEGREE OF FREEDOM REGARDING EXPENDITURES WHICH ENABLES THEM TO MAXIMISE THEIR OWN GOALS.**

7. **MARRIS**[3] developed a model which emphasised **CORPORATE GROWTH AS THE MAIN OBJECTIVE.** The model, as the others discussed so far in this chapter, assumes a separation between management and ownership (shareholders) and a sales market with a low level of competitive activity. It is also assumed in this model that **MANAGERS RELATE THEIR SALARIES AND STATUS TO THE SIZE OF THE FIRM;** any growth in the size of the firm therefore enhances their salaries and status within the firm. They therefore see the **GROWTH OF THE FIRM AS ONE OF THEIR MAJOR OBJECTIVES.** On the other hand they fear takeovers by other firms as this may result in a loss of status and scope for salary increases.

Takeover attempts are deemed to result from a depressed share valuation below the market valuation as judged by the firm considering the takeover. The main source of growth, through internal growth and diversification, depends upon a high level of retained profits for re-investment, however this creates a dilemma because a high level of retentions implies a low level of dividend payments to shareholders which reduces the market valuation of the company. The management is therefore faced with a 'trade-off' situation between the dividend policy and retained profits and must seek the optimal balance between the two. The Valuation Ratio of a company is expressed as:

$$\text{VALUATION RATIO} = \frac{\text{SHARE PRICE VALUATION}}{\text{ACCOUNTING VALUATION (BOOK VALUE)}}$$

and when the valuation ratio falls too low the firm becomes liable to takeover attempts. **THE OBJECTIVE OF THE MANAGEMENT CAN THEREFORE BE SAID TO BE TO MAINTAIN THE MINIMUM VALUATION RATIO CONSISTENT WITH DETERRING TAKEOVER ATTEMPTS IN ORDER TO MAXIMISE GROWTH WHILST RETAINING SECURITY.** Shareholders would prefer the maximisation of the valuation ratio through a higher dividend policy, management however will prefer a higher growth rate.

8. The models discussed so far are generally referred to as **MANAGERIAL THEORIES** of the firm. These models stress the maximisation of some managerial objective although usually it is subject to some constraint. To the extent that they attempt to maximise an objective they have this feature in common with the profit maximising models. Another set of theories of the firm, referred to as **BEHAVIOURAL THEORIES,** which are based on the work of **H.A. SIMON,**[4] recognise that management faced with the complexity of the data and its imperfect nature recognise the impossibility of making the optimal decisions required for maximising behaviour and instead attempt to **"SATISFICE"**. This means that a firm's management will attempt to set itself **MINIMAL STANDARDS OF ACHIEVEMENT INTENDED ONLY TO ENSURE THE FIRM'S SURVIVAL AND A LEVEL OF PROFIT WHICH IS ACCEPTABLE TO SHAREHOLDERS.** Satisficing behaviour is not necessarily static as it involves a learning process. If a firm easily achieves its given objective it will review its aspiration

levels in the following period upwards; failure may result in the stabilisation or lowering of aspirations in the following period.

9. **CYERT AND MARCH**[5] built upon the work of Simon and developed a model in which the firm was viewed as a **COALITION OF DIFFERENT INTEREST GROUPS,** which includes managers, shareholders, employees, the Government, and creditors. These interest groups form a **LOOSE COALITION** but each group within the coalition will have **DIFFERING GOALS WHICH MAY CONFLICT;** these goals will receive attention in sequence as the particular group finds itself in a position to promote its interests according to how important it is perceived to be in the coalition at a particular time. **THE CONFLICT BETWEEN DIFFERENT INTEREST GROUPS IS RESOLVED BY A PROCESS OF CONTINUOUS BARGAINING.** Where groups fail to have their goals satisfied they are compensated by **'SIDE PAYMENTS'** which may be in the form of higher salaries, a higher status in the management structure, or more of the trappings of status such as a larger office or more office furniture etc. Shareholders are seen as a passive group who are easily satisfied, whilst the 'active' management group requires more than just side payments, and this group has most influence on the organisation's objectives. Management does not attempt to maximise profits, or any other variable, but **ATTEMPTS TO ACHIEVE AN ACCEPTABLE LEVEL OF PERFORMANCE FOR A NUMBER OF OPERATIONAL GOALS.** These goals reflect the objectives of different groups in the coalition and frequently conflict. The conflict between groups is resolved by the bargaining process described above. The organisational goals can be briefly summarised as follows:

9.1 **A PRODUCTION GOAL** — production should be relatively stable and should keep the plant fully employed.

9.2 **AN INVENTORY GOAL** — stocks should be maintained at a level which avoids 'stockouts' but without tying up excessive amounts of working capital.

9.3 **A SALES GOAL** — in terms of both revenue and market share, should be increased.

9.4 **A PROFIT GOAL** — should be sufficient to finance investment for growth, dividends, and internal budgets.

The goals which are actually pursued will be a **COMPROMISE REFLECTING THE WAY IN WHICH CONFLICTS ARE RESOLVED WITHIN THE PARTICULAR ORGANISATION.** Provided that goals are satisfactorily achieved within one period then the same goals may be pursued in the following period. This satisficing behaviour gives rise to the possibility of **ORGANISATIONAL SLACK.** Organisational slack refers to the situation where the firm has **MORE RESOURCES AVAILABLE THAN ARE NECESSARY TO MEET CURRENT GOALS.** This serves several functions, firstly more resources are available for making side payments in order to resolve unsettled conflict within the organisation, and secondly during unfavourable market conditions the firm can reduce the level of organisational slack in order to maintain satisfactory performance levels. **THE PRESENCE OF ORGANISATIONAL SLACK ENABLES THE FIRM TO REMAIN STABLE AND THEREFORE VIABLE.**

10. Observation in the real world suggests that businessmen frequently have little knowledge of their marginal costs and are not therefore in a position to make the optimal price and output decisions necessary for profit maximising theories. The managerial and behavioural theories attempt to overcome these weaknesses by making a different set of assumptions about the ways in which firms actually behave, and the prediction of these models are frequently consistent with the actual behaviour observed within large companies.

SELF ASSESSMENT QUESTIONS

1. Explain what is meant by Satisficing Behaviour.

2. Discuss the effect of sales maximisation with a profit constraint on the output of the firm.

3. Discuss growth as a corporate objective.

4. What are the means by which goals are established in the Cyert and March model?

REFERENCES

1. Baumol, W.J., Business Behaviour, Value and Growth, Macmillan, New York, 1959.
2. Williamson, O.E., The Economics of Discretionary Behaviour: Managerial Objectives in a Theory of the Firm, Prentice-Hall, 1964.
3. Marris, R., The Economic Theory of Managerial Capitalism, Freepress, Glencoe, ILL, 1964.
4. Simon, H.A., Theories of Decision Making in Economics, American Economic Review, Vol. XLIX, June 1959.
5. Cyert, R.M. and March, J.G., A Behavioural Theory of the Firm, Prentice-Hall, 1963.

Chapter 21

THE PRICE MECHANISM

1. This chapter extends the discussion of the price mechanism in Chapter 1. It will be recalled that the basic problems facing society are those of **WHAT** to produce, **HOW** to produce it, and **FOR WHOM** the goods are to be produced. In a free market economy these problems are solved automatically by the interplay of market forces. According to Adam Smith "each individual following his own self interest unknowingly brings about the general good", and the problems of what, how, and for whom are solved by what Smith referred to as the 'invisible hand' of the price mechanism.

2. Consumer sovereignty is said to prevail in a market economy because production and therefore resource allocation is in accordance with the preferences of consumers as expressed in the market place. If consumers prefer a good they will purchase more of it i.e. it receives more 'consumer votes', as demand increases the market price will rise, and these 'price signals' indicate to producers which goods should be produced in greater quantities.

3. As the demand for goods changes so too does their relative prices, which results in a reallocation of the factors of production.

DIAGRAM 21.1

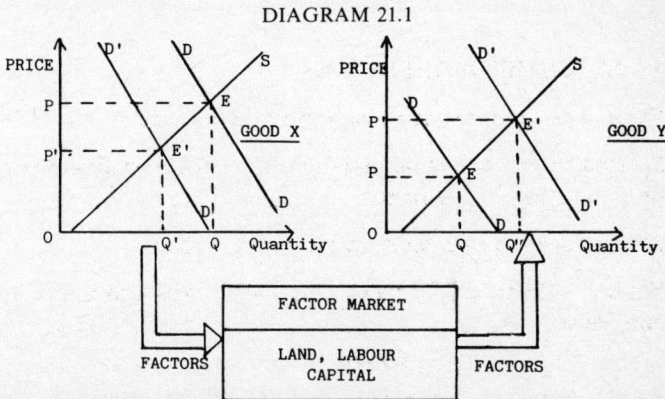

In Diagram 21.1, assuming good X and Y are close substitutes, and there is a change in consumers' preferences away from X and in favour of Y. The price of X falls to P′ and the price of Y rises to P′. The increase in Y indicates to entrepreneurs that Y is more profitable to produce and a transfer of resources will take place through demand and supply on the factor market and more of Y will be produced. Output and resource allocation has been in accordance with the preferences of consumers as indicated by the 'price signals'.

4.   The concept of consumer sovereignty in the modern economy has been challenged by several writers, but in particular by J.K. Galbraith. Galbraith argues that consumer sovereignty is a myth and that the large corporations are in fact sovereign as they are able to create wants and impose them upon consumers by the use of advertising. Even if this overstates the case it is at least probable that advertising distorts consumers' preferences. Opponents of this view point to examples where consumers have resisted the attempts of large corporations to manipulate their preferences, in particular the failure of the Ford Motor Company to market their Edsel model in the 1950's.

5.   For the price mechanism to operate efficiently it is necessary for the conditions of perfect competition to exist. In reality there are imperfections in the vast majority of markets, the majority being either oligopolistic or monopolistic, and therefore, resource allocation in these markets will also be less than perfect.

6.   The market may fail to provide certain goods which society considers to be so essential that they should be provided free of charge. Such goods typically include education and medicine. Because such goods are considered to be so meritorious to society they are referred to as '**MERIT GOODS**'.

7.   Another class of goods which the price mechanism would fail to supply in adequate quantities is referred to as '**PURE PUBLIC GOODS**'. The essential characteristics of such goods are:

7.1   They are **NON RIVAL IN CONSUMPTION** i.e. if one person consumes more it does not mean that there is less for others as is the case with normal goods.

7.2   They are in **JOINT SUPPLY** i.e. if the supply is increased it is increased to everyone.

7.3   They are **NON-EXCLUDABLE** i.e. nobody can be prevented from consuming them.

The classical examples of such goods are: light from a lighthouse, law and order, and defence. The characteristics of such goods make it impossible to charge a user price. If a rational consumer was asked to reveal his preferences for such goods and state how much he was prepared to pay for them he would say zero because he would assume that he would receive all he wanted anyway. However, if each individual responded in the same way then there would be none provided, or at least there would be under provision, a problem referred to as the 'free-rider' problem; which makes it impossible to make provision of such goods by a system of user prices. The only way such goods can be provided is collectively by Governments through the tax system.

8.   Market prices fail to reflect **SOCIAL COSTS** and **BENEFITS**. Social costs may also be referred to as **EXTERNALITIES** or **SPILLOVERS**. These occur when **ACTIONS BY ONE PARTY CREATE COSTS WHICH ARE BORNE BY OTHERS;** or by society as a whole. The act of production will involve private costs for the entrepreneur, but pollution in the form of smoke or effluent will impose costs upon the community at large. In a similar manner private expenditures, on for example health, education and housing may create benefits not only to the individual but to society as a whole, for example; innoculations provide a private benefit to the individual but there is also the benefit to other individuals who will

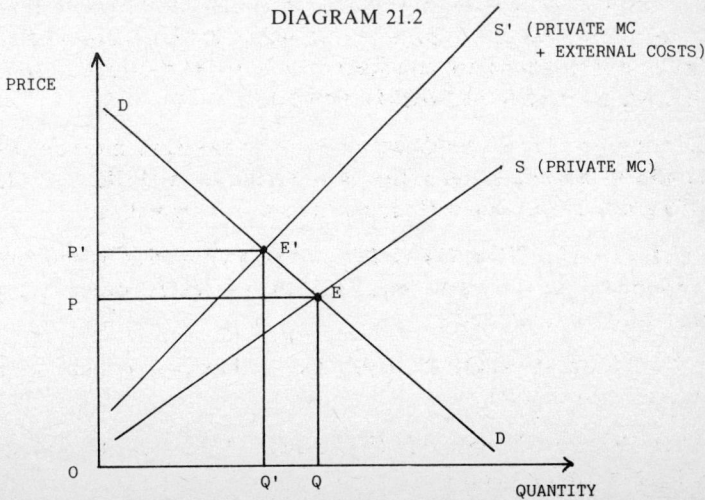

DIAGRAM 21.2

PRICE

D

S' (PRIVATE MC
     + EXTERNAL COSTS)

S (PRIVATE MC)

P'   E'

P   E

D

O   Q'   Q   QUANTITY

not now be at risk of catching the disease. **MARKET PRICES MAY THEREFORE FAIL TO REFLECT THESE EXTERNAL COSTS AND BENEFITS AND WILL NOT BRING ABOUT AN OPTIMAL ALLOCATION OF RESOURCES.**

In Diagram 21.2 when only private costs are taken into account equilibrium price is P and quantity is Q, this does not however reflect the extra cost to society as a whole, or the **MARGINAL SOCIAL COST.** If social costs are included the supply curve, or marginal cost curve, becomes S′ with the higher price P′ and lower output Q′. These external costs are unlikely to be incorporated in the decision making of a private firm or individual as they will not be concerned with the effect of the marginal cost of their activites upon society as a whole, resulting in over production of the good i.e. Q instead of Q′. **THE PROBLEM IS THEREFORE HOW TO MAKE INDIVIDUALS AND FIRMS INCORPORATE SOCIAL COSTS INTO THEIR DECISION MAKING** or how to **INTERNALISE** them.

Some commentators such as E.J. Mishan suggest the use of the tax system in the form of providing subsidies where there are external benefits, and taxes where there are costs, in order to bring about a level of output which is optimal for society as a whole. In diagram 21.3 market price is P and quantity Q. If there are external costs however the supply curve does not reflect the true marginal cost of

DIAGRAM 21.3

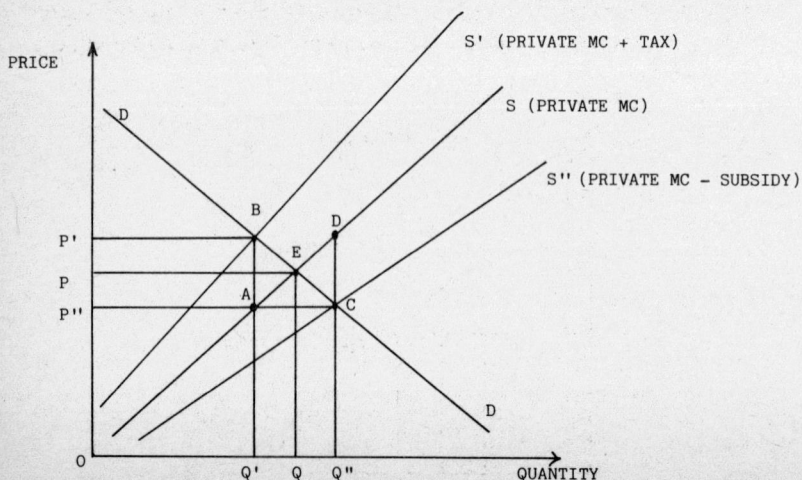

production and the imposition of a tax raises the producer's costs to reflect both the private production costs and the external costs to society. As a consequence the price rises to P' and output falls to the optimal output for society, Q'. Where there are external benefits private production costs do not reflect the benefits to society and the provision of a subsidy to the producer reduces his costs, price falls to P'' and output increases to Q'', with more of the socially desirable good produced. Provided the tax or subsidy is equal to the value of the externality the result should be optimal for society as a whole. In the diagram the tax would be A-B and the subsidy C-D in order to achieve the socially optimal outputs.

9.   As mentioned in Chapter 1, criticism of the price mechanism on the basis of unequal income distribution is not a valid criticism of the price mechanism, as the price mechanism and income distribution are separate issues.

10.   The concept of **CONSUMER'S SURPLUS** refers to the **DIFFERENCE BETWEEN THE TOTAL UTILITY THE CONSUMER RECEIVES AND THE TOTAL MARKET VALUE.** This surplus arises because the consumer pays a price on all the units he purchases which is equal to the price of the last unit, however we know from the Law of Declining Marginal Utility that the earlier units are valued more highly than the last. The consumer will spend his budget on a good up to the point where **PRICE = MARGINAL UTILITY (P = MU) ONLY;** after this point he will purchase no more as he has maximised his utility. The concept is illustrated in diagram

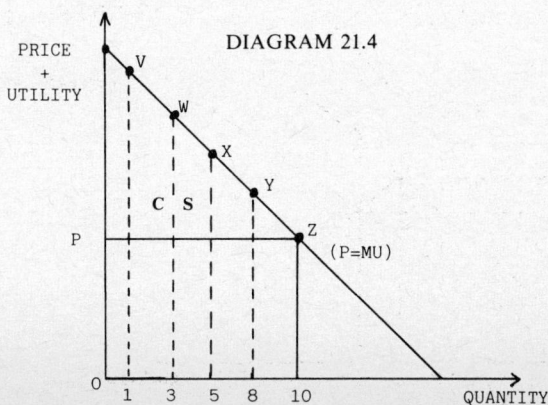

DIAGRAM 21.4

21.4. The consumer pays price P for 10 units, however had only 1 unit been available the consumer would have paid price V, if 3 had been available price W, and so on. Only for the tenth unit is the $P = MU$, a surplus of marginal utility over price being gained by the consumer on all of the earlier units. The area of the triangle above P-Z is the **CONSUMER'S SURPLUS**. At the tenth unit the consumer's evaluation of the marginal utility he receives from the additional unit is equal to the price, and total utility is maximised.

11. **PRODUCER'S SURPLUS** is the excess of market price over the minimum that would be necessary to persuade the producer to produce a given quantity. As the minimum return required to produce a given quantity is the marginal cost (MC), the **PRODUCER'S SURPLUS IS THE DIFFERENCE BETWEEN MARKET PRICE AND MARGINAL COST.** As the marginal cost can be equated with the entrepreneur's opportunity cost then **PRODUCER'S SURPLUS IS EQUIVALENT TO THE SURPLUS OVER OPPORTUNITY COST.** As the competitive firm's marginal cost curve is also its supply curve we can use the firm's supply curve to illustrate the point. In diagram 21.5 market price is P and quantity

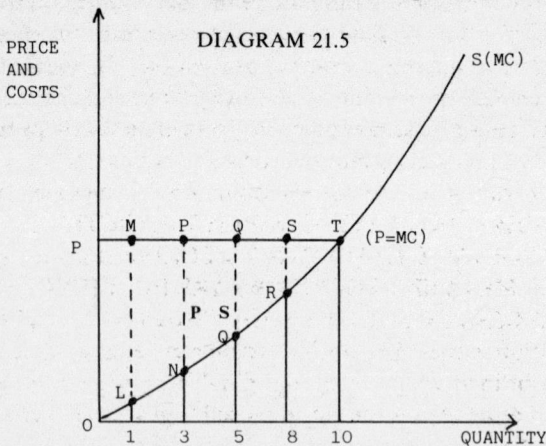

DIAGRAM 21.5

10. For the first unit however MC is L but price P is received, L-M is therefore the producer's surplus. For the third unit it is N-P, and so on. Only for the tenth unit is the market price exactly equal to the marginal cost, i.e. **P = MC.** The firm will not produce more than 10 because the MC would exceed the price received. Producer's surplus is therefore maximised at 10 units, and is represented by the triangle OPT.

PRICE
AND
COSTS

DIAGRAM 21.6

S($\sum$ MC)

AC

CS

P=MU=MC

$\overline{P}$

PS

O

10

QUANTITY

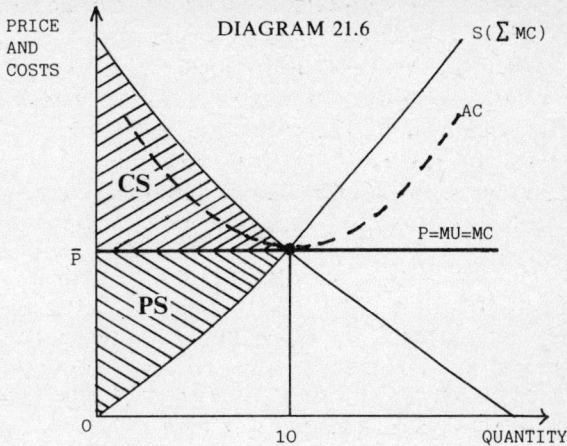

12.   If we assume a perfectly competitive industry it is possible to demonstrate that the competitive model can achieve optimal allocative efficiency. In diagram 21.6, the two previous diagrams are combined to illustrate a competitive market in equilibrium. We assume now that the demand and supply curves are market demand and supply curves. The market price P and quantity 10 maximises the total area of producer's and consumer's surplus. At this price each firm is operating at the lowest point on its average cost curve, **CONSUMERS ARE PAYING A PRICE EXACTLY EQUAL TO THE MARGINAL UTILITY THEY RECEIVE FROM THE LAST UNIT (P = MU) AND PRODUCERS ARE RECEIVING EXACTLY THE MARGINAL COST OF PRODUCING THAT UNIT (P = MC).** The situation is therefore optimal for society as a whole. It is for the reasons outlined above that marginal cost pricing is frequently advocated as a rule for the Nationalised Industries to follow in their pricing policies.

13.   Given the existence of perfect competition in all markets it is theoretically possible for an allocation of resources to be achieved which is optimal for society as a whole. In reality however this conclusion has to be seriously qualified in order to take into account the deficiencies in the price mechanism as it operates in the modern economy, and the broader requirements of society as a whole.

SELF ASSESSMENT QUESTIONS

1. What is meant by consumer sovereignty?

2. How does the market mechanism allocate society's resources?

3. What are the characteristics of 'pure public goods'?

4. Distinguish between private costs and social costs.

5. What is the 'free-rider' problem?

6. What are the market imperfections which prevent the price mechanism from achieving an optimal allocation of resources?

INDEX

ADDITIONAL READING

Donaldson, P., 10 x Economics (Penguin 1982).

Harvey, J., Modern Economics, 4th Edition (Macmillan, 1983).

Kermally, S., Multiple Choice Economics, 1st Edition
    (Checkmate/Arnold, 1985).

Keynes, J.M., The General Theory of Employment, Interest and
    Money (Macmillan, 1981).

Lancaster, K., Modern Economics, Principles and Policy,
    2nd Edition (Rand McNally, 1979).

Levick, J., Essential Topics for Examinations in Economics,
    1st Edition (Checkmate/Arnold, 1985).

Lipsey, R.G., An Introduction to Positive Economics, 6th Edition
    (Weidenfeld & Nicolson, 1983).

Livesey, F., A Textbook of Economics, (Polytech Publishers, 1978).

Prest, A.R. & Coppock, D.J., The UK Economy: A Manual of
    Applied Economics, 9th Edition (Weidenfeld & Nicolson, 1982).

Samuelson, P.S., Economics, 11th Edition (McGraw-Hill, 1980).

Stanlake, G.F., Introductory Economics, 3rd Edition
    (Longman 1981).

Whitehead, G., Economics Made Simple (Heinemann, 1982).

Students should also attempt to keep abreast of developments by reading current periodicals such as The Economist, Bank Reviews and the Economic Progress Report published by the Treasury (available from the Publication Division, Central Office of Information, Hercules Road, London, SE1 7DU).

Useful sources of statistics are:—
    Economic Trends
    Annual Abstract of Statistics
    National Income and Expenditure
These publications are available in most libraries and give a comprehensive coverage of relevant statistics.

THE BASIC CONCEPTS SERIES

The Basic Concepts series attempts to explain in a clear and concise manner the main concepts involved in a subject. Paragraphs are numbered for ease of reference and key points are emboldened for clear identification, with self assessment questions at the end of each chapter. The texts should prove useful to students studying for A level, professional and first year degree courses. Other titles in the series include:—

QUESTIONS AND ANSWERS SERIES

These highly successful revision aids contain questions and answers based on actual examination questions and provide fully worked answers for each question. The books are written by experienced lecturers and examiners and will be useful for students preparing for O and A level, foundation and BTEC examinations. Subjects include:—

Economics by G. Walker
Accounting by T. Hines
Multiple Choice Economics by Dr. S. Kermally
O level Mathematics by R.H. Evans
A level Pure Mathematics and Statistics by R.H. Evans
A level Pure and Applied Mathematics by R.H. Evans
O level Physics by R.H. Evans
O level Chemistry by J. Sheen
O level Human Biology by D. Reese